GREAT WOMEN OF THE BIBLE

GREAT WOMEN
OF THE BIBLE

By
CLARENCE EDWARD MACARTNEY

ABINGDON PRESS
NEW YORK ● NASHVILLE

GREAT WOMEN OF THE BIBLE

Copyright MCMXLII by Whitmore & Stone

Library of Congress Catalog Card Number: 42-20130

N

SET UP, PRINTED, AND BOUND BY THE
PARTHENON PRESS, AT NASHVILLE,
TENNESSEE, UNITED STATES OF AMERICA

FOREWORD

I HAVE PREACHED FREQUENTLY ON THE GREAT MEN of the Bible. Some of these sermons appear in the volumes *The Greatest Men of the Bible* and *Sermons on Old Testament Heroes,* and here and there in others. But until recently I had never preached on the great women of the Bible. Quite often I have received requests to do so, but I had some doubts in my mind as to such a course of sermons. It did not seem at first that the narratives of the women of the Bible had enough of the personal and dramatic element in them to make them the subjects of successful and popular sermons.

But last winter, in answer to many requests, the congregation was given an opportunity to vote on the greatest women of the Bible, just as it had voted on the greatest men. In that vote Ruth stood first in the list, and Eve last. Most of the women dealt with in this volume were on the list of those who received the highest number of votes. However, I have added several women who did not receive a place in the first ten.

As I began to study these characters and to prepare and then preach the sermons, I was agreeably surprised at the way the subject opened up. If anything, the sermons on the great women of the

Bible proved more popular than the sermons on the great men of the Bible.

Among the subjects of the sermons in this volume is one of the bad women of the Bible, for no series on women of the Bible would be complete without a sermon on such a character as Delilah, the temptress of Samson.

To preach on these Biblical women is to illustrate life in its deep reality—sometimes base, ignoble, contemptible, and wicked, but ofttimes lofty, noble, godlike, and glorious. Like the great men of the Bible, too, the great women of the Bible afford the preacher an unsurpassed opportunity to press home upon the people the claims of Christ as Friend and Redeemer.

CLARENCE EDWARD MACARTNEY.

CONTENTS

I

THE WOMAN WHO GOT HER MAN

"Thy God shall be my God."

RUTH 1:16

IN THE VOTE OF THE CONGREGATION ON THE TEN greatest women of the Bible, Ruth stood first, and Eve, the first in historical order, stood last. In certain respects I was somewhat surprised at the popularity of Ruth. I had thought that Mary, Sarah, Hannah, Rebekah, or Rachel would take the first place. But the vote was for Ruth.

Why did so many vote for Ruth? Was it because she was an ancestress of our Lord? Was it because of her touching and unusual loyalty to her mother-in-law Naomi? Was it because of the story of how she won Boaz for her husband by that unusual night courtship on the threshing floor? Was it because she firmly and forever chose God and the people of God as her God and her people? Or was it because of the simple beauty and charm of her person and character? I suppose that all of these things entered into the choice of the voters. The Book of Ruth is one of the briefest of the Bible, but the portrait it gives us of this Moabitish damsel

[9]

who came back a young widow to Bethlehem with afflicted and unhappy Naomi is unforgettable.

When Benjamin Franklin was abroad as our representative in Europe, he would sometimes gather together a fashionable company, and telling them that he had come upon a most remarkable piece of Oriental literature, read to them the Book of Ruth. When he had finished, all would express their great delight and ask him how he came upon such a gem of literature. Then he would tell them it was in the Bible. Perhaps some of you have never read the Book of Ruth. If so, I envy you the surprise and joy which are in store for you if you take the trouble, and the few minutes required, to read this great little book.

The story of Ruth is an idyl of domestic love which comes between the books of Judges and Samuel, so filled with war and murder and cruelty. It is a sweet interlude of peace and love in a fierce, wild chorus of war and passion. In this book not a single wicked, cruel, or licentious person makes his appearence. Here we behold the attractiveness of virtue, the beauty of sacrifice, and the winsomeness of simple trust in God.

A TALE OF THREE WIDOWS

The story of Ruth is a tale of three widows. Out of Bethlehem, where Christ was to be born, driven by the famine, Elimelech, his wife Naomi, and their two sons, Mahlon and Chilion, had migrated, not westward, as families and races have done through the ages, but eastward, across the Jordan to the land of Moab, where God was not known. But in that land they were doomed to disappointment. Life was even harder there than it had been in Bethlehem. First Elimelech, the head of the family, sickened and died. And then, ten years after, the two sons died, leaving Naomi alone with her two heathen daughters-in-law, Orpah and Ruth. Sorrow as well as joy turns the heart homeward and to the scenes of youth. It was not strange, then, that in her sorrow Naomi turned homeward to Bethlehem. Her two daughters-in-law determined to go with her; but when they came to the river Jordan, the dividing line between the two countries, Naomi, beautiful and unselfish, besought the two young widows to go back to Moab. They could not know as she did, she told them, how hard life was in a strange land. Moreover, it would be difficult for them to find husbands in Bethlehem. If they went with her, they would share those sorrows which God had brought upon them. Hearing that, Orpah kissed her mother and turned back to Moab. But Ruth clave to her. She answered Naomi in these immortal words—and what she said ranks among the most beautiful sayings of all the Bible—"Entreat me not to leave thee, or to return from following after thee: for whither thou goest, I will go; and where thou lodgest, I will lodge: thy people shall be my people, and thy God my God: where thou diest, will I die, and there will I be buried: the Lord do so to me, and more also, if aught but death part thee and me." Sometimes, where it seems appropriate, I use that matchless affirmation of Ruth in the marriage service. Indeed, that last phrase, "If aught but death part thee and me," is the origin of the familiar marriage affirmation, "Till death us do part."

A PRETTY GLEANER IN THE FIELDS

There had been great changes in Bethlehem during the years of Naomi's absence in Moab. When the familiar landmarks came into view I imagine her heart beat high with hope. There again was her native land and her native village. But there were sad memories too. She recalled the day she had set out with her family for Moab with great expectations of the future. People did not migrate much in those days, and the departure or the return to or from a far country was an event in the monotonous life of the village. The whole town turned out when they heard that Naomi was coming home. They remembered her as the young and beautiful wife of Elimelech, the fairest woman in the village. But when they saw this travel-stained woman with the marks of sorrow and advancing years upon her, they could hardly believe it was Naomi. "Is this Naomi?" the villagers said one to another as they gathered around her and looked upon her faded beauty. Naomi means "Pleasantness." But Naomi, recognizing the change in her person and her lot, answered the wondering women: "Call me not Naomi, call me Mara [Bitterness] : for the Almighty hath dealt very bitterly with me. I went out full, and the Lord hath brought me home again empty: why then call ye me Naomi?" Although she had met with adversity and misfortune, Naomi was not soured or embittered by her lot, for she reverently recognized the hand of God in her life.

They were harvesting the barley at Bethlehem when Naomi and Ruth returned. The harvest was, and still is, the one great social and economic event in that land where men must have bread.

If the villagers had wondered at the faded charms of Naomi, they had not failed to mark the fair and womanly grace of the Moabitish damsel who accompanied her. Although of a foreign, idol-worshiping race, Ruth soon made friends among her new people whose lot and God she had chosen. There were no men in the household to go into the fields and toil, and they had no fields of their own where others could toil for them. But Ruth, realizing the situation, and Naomi's and her own need, asked permission of her mother-in-law to go into the fields and glean after the reapers.

The Old Testament was by no means all law and severity. Strands of mercy and compassion ran through the fabric of the Hebrew jurisprudence, and one of those strands was the law of the harvest that the poor and the needy could glean after the reapers and gather what was necessary for their sustenance. The corners of the fields were not to be wholly gleaned, nor the fruit trees picked or beaten twice. Always something was to be left for the foreigner and the poor. Both poor and a foreigner, Ruth was certain of consideration at the hands of the reapers.

Ruth could not have known that morning all that it was to mean to her; but when she went forth to glean it was her hap, or, as we would say, her good fortune, to light upon that part of the field belonging to Boaz, who was connected by blood with the family of Naomi's husband. She had hoped and prayed that wherever she gleaned in the fields she might find favor in the eyes of some kindhearted man. Her prayer was answered.

There is Ruth, then, following the reapers up and down the fields of Boaz. If you have seen the reapers and the threshers at work in Palestine, it will not be difficult for you to picture the scene, or even if you have paintings or photographs of it.

What strikes one today is the variety of the colors worn by the women. As I remember it now, yellow, red, and blue were the prevailing colors, the head-dress of the women being the most conspicuous part of their attire. I fancy that Ruth did not forget to array herself in the most becoming colors that morning when she went forth to glean, and that Naomi took a hand, too, and tried this or that scarf about Ruth's head and brow before they finally decided upon the one which best suited her style of beauty. From what follows it is plain that they made no mistake.

In his beautiful "Ode to a Nightingale," John Keats imagines Ruth listening to the entrancing song of that bird in the fields at Bethlehem:

Perhaps the self-same song that found a path
Through the sad heart of Ruth, when, sick for home,
She stood in tears amid the alien corn.

But I think Keats missed it when he spoke of Ruth as "sick for home." Ruth had willingly and gladly chosen Israel and turned her back on Moab and its idols forever.

As the day advances, here come the mowers swinging their sickles, and the reapers gathering up the grain and binding it into bundles, just as men did from the dawn of history, until one day a young farmer in Rockbridge County, Virginia,

[15]

had an idea, and the reaper was invented. Today on the campus of Washington and Lee University at Lexington there stands a monument to that young man, Cyrus McCormick, and on the monument are cut these words, "He lifted the burden from the back of labor." At length Boaz appears on the scene to see how the work progresses. The greetings which passed between employer and employees showed the character of Boaz and the happy relationship which existed. "The Lord be with you," Boaz said to the reapers, who answered, "The Lord bless thee."

A WOMAN PROPOSES

Boaz may have been a bachelor, and perhaps well along in years, but he did not fail to note the presence of the strange damsel, and looked upon her with admiring eye as he watched her bend her lithesome young body with infinite grace as she gleaned after the reapers. Calling the foreman to him, Boaz said to him, "Who is that damsel?" When he was told that it was the Moabitish girl who had come back with Naomi, he called her to him and told her not to glean elsewhere, but to stay in his fields, where she would receive every consideration. When Ruth expressed surprise that she had found such grace in his eyes, Boaz said to her that he had heard of her kindness and loyalty to her mother-in-law and

[16]

prayed that God would bless her. In beautiful language he said, "A full reward be given thee of the Lord God of Israel, under whose wings thou art come to trust." When Ruth went back to join the reapers, Boaz charged them to deal kindly with her, and in addition to what was generally left, to drop some "handfuls of purpose" for her to glean. The result was that when Ruth went back that night to Naomi she took with her a ephah of barley. And much more than an ephah of barley, too: Ruth carried home the heart of Boaz; for wisely, unlike Whittier's judge, who saw Maud Muller in the meadow and sighed, and rode by, Boaz appeared at the field every day Ruth came to glean.

Naomi asked her where she had gleaned; and when Ruth told her it was in the field of Boaz, Naomi, knowing that Boaz was a kinsman of her husband, cried out in joy, "Blessed be he of the Lord, who hath not left off his kindness to the living and to the dead." Every day Ruth went to glean in the fields of Boaz, and every day Boaz saw her and his heart warmed toward her.

At length, one day as the harvest season was drawing to a close, the wise Naomi, seeing that Boaz was fond of Ruth, and that Ruth herself was not unwilling, made to Ruth the suggestion that she go to Boaz and ask him to marry her. We must view that plan and plot of Naomi in the light of the ancient custom that if a man died leaving his wife, and without a child, it was the duty of the nearest kinsman to marry her. Ruth's dead husband, Mahlon or Chilion, whichever it was, was a kinsman of Boaz, and this fact lay back of Naomi's plot. It would certainly be awkward, and often unpleasant, if law and custom required men to marry the widows of their relatives, for all are not like Ruth. But in those days the continuity of the family and the nation, rather than the individual, was the great thing.

4;10

Following the directions of Naomi, Ruth arrayed herself in her most attractive garments; and that night after Boaz had lain down to sleep on one of his threshing floors, a custom still followed in order to guard the grain against theft, she came softly down to the threshing floor. In a part of the floor removed from the others Boaz lay sleeping. Silently Ruth made her way in her bare feet over the soft piles of the grain, stopping now and then and sinking down with fear when one of the sleeping reapers stirred uneasily in his slumber, until at length she came to where Boaz slept, and lay down at his feet.

At midnight Boaz awoke and, turning himself, was amazed and frightened to see a woman lying at his feet. "Who art thou?" he exclaimed. Ruth replied: "I am Ruth thine handmaid: spread therefore thy skirt over thine handmaid; for thou art a near kinsman." When Boaz heard that, his heart

[18]

leaped with joy that Ruth had been unmindful of the many young men nearer her own age and had set her affections upon him.

Boaz was immediately willing. But his first thought was for the good name of Ruth and for his own good name; and that should be uppermost in the mind of every man and every woman. He told Ruth that if a kinsman nearer to her than he was would not marry her, he would gladly do so. That they could ascertain when the day came. It would not do that the reapers should know that a woman had come by night to the threshing floor. That might ruin the reputation of both of them. He therefore told her to lie quiet till the day was beginning to break. Then, when it was still dark enough so that no one could be recognized, Ruth arose, and taking with her six measures of grain that the generous Boaz had poured into her veil, left the threshing floor and returned to her mother in law

Ruth's plan was a bold one, and had certain dangers; but it worked well and Ruth got her man, and never did a woman get a better one; for Boaz was a man of high sense of honor, a virtuous man, a godly man, a generous man, and a kind man. Young women who are following in the steps of Ruth and seeking a husband would do well to consider if the man in question has some of the traits of Boaz.

A faint heart never won a fair husband. All's well that ends well. Probably Boaz, the old bachelor, would never have had the courage himself to seek the hand of Ruth. That night God worked in a mysterious way his wonders to perform. But two hearts were made happy. A true godly home was established, and a child was born and a son was given. They called his name Obed. He became the father of Jesse, and Jesse was the father of David, and of the line of David came Christ.

PROVIDENCE AND HUMAN LIFE

This famous story yields two great and timeless truths. The first of these is the fact of God's providence in our life. Every one of the characters of the Book of Ruth reverently owns the presence of God in life and human affairs: Naomi who saw the hand of God in her sorrow and adversity; Boaz who recognized the hand of God in the good fortune that gave him Ruth for a wife; and Ruth herself who, as Boaz expressed it, put her trust under the wings of the Lord God of Israel.

The record reads that when Ruth went out that morning to glean, "her hap was to light on a part of the field belonging unto Boaz." The whole story with its great sequence turns upon that hap, that chance. Had it been some other field, the history would have been different. But it was the field of

Boaz, the kinsman of her dead husband's family. Through that hap Ruth became the ancestress of Jesus Christ, the Saviour of her soul and the Redeemer of mankind. Great events turn upon the hinges of little happenings. Ruth could not have told why, when she went forth that morning to glean and looked over the fields where the reapers were at work, she turned to the left or right and chose the field belonging to Boaz. With her it was only a happenso. But God was with her. God guided her footsteps that morning.

When you look back you see how life has been made up of happenings like that. Had you gone east instead of west, taken a morning train instead of an evening train, gone around another corner, met another person, life could not have been what it has been. Faith will recognize God's hand not only in the obviously pleasant things of life, such as the bringing together of Ruth and Boaz, but also in what are termed the hard things of life. As life wore on for Robert Louis Stevenson, his faith became stronger in what he called "the kindness of the scheme of things and the goodness of our veiled God." To his father he wrote:

There is a fine text in the Bible, I don't know where,[1] to the effect that all things work together for good to those who love the Lord. . . . . Strange as it may seem

[1] Romans 8:28.

to you, everything has been, in one way or another, bringing me a little nearer to what I think you would like me to be. . . . . 'Tis a strange world, indeed, but there is a manifest God for those who care to look for Him.

And a greater than Stevenson said:

> There's a divinity that shapes our ends,
> Rough-hew them how we will.[2]

DECISION AND DESTINY

The other great truth which the Book of Ruth illustrates so dramatically is the power of choice and decision. Ruth chose definitely and forever the people of God. Her decision was given in that immortal declaration, "Entreat me not to leave thee: . . . . thy people shall be my people, and thy God my God." When Naomi announced her intention to go back to Bethlehem, both of her daughters-in-law said they would go with her, and both started back with her. But when they reached the boundary line between the two countries, the river Jordan, Orpah yielded to the entreaties of Naomi and, kissing her mother-in-law, went back to Moab. She represents a common type. They abound in all our churches: young women who have some real desire to go with Christ and his people, but who never bring themselves to the point of breaking with the world. Their

[2] William Shakespeare, *Hamlet,* V, 2.

[22]

hearts are in Moab, and eventually back to Moab they go.

But Ruth stands for those whose decision is final and irrevocable. There is no turning back, no backward look even, toward Moab, toward the life of the world. There she stands on the bank of the river Jordan, with her back to Moab, and on her lips that grand decision and choice, "Whither thou goest, I will go; . . . . thy people shall be my people, and thy God my God." Decision, choice, that is the first step in the Christian life. Have you taken that step? Have you made that decision? Have you chosen Jesus Christ and Eternal Life? Great things hung that day on Ruth's choice, and not less great—even the destiny of an immortal soul—hang upon your decision. Will you say the word now, while all the angels listen and all the redeemed give thanks—say it to Him who loved you and died for you, "Entreat me not to leave thee, or to return from following after thee"

II

THE WOMAN WHOSE BEAUTY SAVED A RACE

"And if I perish, I perish."
ESTHER 4:16

"BEAUTY," THE WISE MAN SAID, "IS VAIN." BUT it is not always so. Not when beauty of face and body is joined to beauty of soul. There is a beauty which can inflame and destroy men. History tells of one woman whose beauty dyed the seas with blood and almost destroyed two nations. That was the disastrous influence of the beauty of Helen of Troy—

. . . . the face that launch'd a thousand ships,
And burnt the topless towers of Ilium.[1]

But here we have the story of how God used the beauty of one woman to save a nation from destruction and carry forward his eternal purpose.

The story of Esther is a drama that opens with a banquet which for wickedness and beauty and splendor and length of time has rarely, if ever, been surpassed. It is midnight in the palace of

[1] Christopher Marlowe, *Doctor Faustus,* scene xiv.

Ahasuerus, the king of Persia and the despot of the world. By some he has been identified with that Xerxes who crossed the Hellespont with a great army, forced the pass at Thermopylae and then marched on south through Greece, only to see his invasion checked and his fleet destroyed at the battle of Salamis Bay. I have visited the rocky eminence near Salamis where Xerxes sat and watched his fleet perish in the waters of the Aegean.

> A king sate on the rocky brow
>   Which looks o'er sea-born Salamis;
> And ships, by thousands, lay below,
>   And men and nations;—all were his!
> He counted them at break of day—
> And when the sun set where were they? [2]

Ahasuerus sits in royal state at the center of the table in the great banqueting hall, and all about him are ranged the one hundred and twenty-seven princes of his far-flung empire. This convocation of the satraps of Ahasuerus probably took place at the very time when he was planning his ill-starred invasion of Greece. For one hundred and eighty days, or six months, the king has been engaged in showing these assembled satraps the riches of his glorious kingdom and the honor of his excellent majesty. For the last seven days a great banquet has been in operation. Ahasuerus is flanked by his one hundred

[2] Byron, *Don Juan,* iii, 87.

and twenty-seven princes, all gorgeously arrayed in their resplendent robes, with their gems and jewels and tiaras flashing in the light that glows from the myriad candles and the vast candelabra that hang from the ceiling. The floor of the banquet hall is of black, white, blue, and red marble. Marble columns hold up the roof, from which is suspended a vast canopy of blue, green, and white velvet, fastened with cords of fine linen to silver rings inserted in the marble columns. The beds, or couches, on which the revelers recline are in keeping with the splendor of all else that night, for they are of silver or gold, decorated with the beasts and deities of Persian superstition and wickedness. Every cup out of which the banqueters are drinking is of purest gold, and each cup wrought and chased with a different design.

Slaves and eunuchs, black as the marble tiles of the palace floor, pass to and fro with the viands and the liquors. In the minstrels' galleries sensuous music floats down, with the strains of the harp, bulbul, psaltery, timbrel, flute, cornet, sackbut, and dulcimer mingling their strains. Fountains throw their silver spray up from their basins, and the sweet incense of Persia, India, and Ormuz fills the air. On a central platform dancing girls, their flimsy garments disclosing the wanton beauty of their bodies, whirl beguilingly about in the Oriental dance. Seven days have passed, and they are still eating and drinking and dancing. Many have been overcome by drink and fatigue and are being carried out by their slaves on litters. Ahasuerus is thinking to himself, "What more can I do to entertain and excite these guests?" Then to his alcohol-inflamed brain comes a new idea. "The queen! The beauty of all the earth! I will bring in Vashti and display her beauty to my satraps and their ladies." Summoning his seven chamberlains, Mehuman, Carcas, Zethar, and the others, he commands them in his drunken voice to bring in Vashti.

It is not without significance that the sacred chronicler records that it was when the heart of Ahasuerus was inflamed with wine that he made his shameful and infamous proposal concerning Vashti the queen. That is the old, old history of strong drink, ever since it left Noah, God-fearing Noah, uncovered and debauched in the presence of his sons, and by the very altar which he had built to God. However commonplace and fashionable it may be to drink liquor, let it be remembered that the effect of liquor is to stir up the lower passions of one's nature and to relax the soul's watch over its safety. In a moment of such relaxation, when the stimulation of strong drink has weakened the natural resistance to evil, young men and young women have written a record of sorrow or of shame which can never be reversed.

Startled by so wicked and unprecedented a proposal, the drunken lords sit up in eagerness to await the coming of the far-famed queen. But they were doomed to disappointment, and Ahasuerus to futile rage; for Vashti refused to come in. She refused to expose herself to the lascivious gaze of Ahasuerus and his drink-inflamed satraps. Vashti said "No"— one of the great God-inspired "Noes" of all history. Let all women remember that "No." Vashti had world-famed beauty; but she lives forever in history, not because she had beauty, but because she had character, had respect for herself, without which the fairest beauty is but as a jewel in a swine's snout. She counted the cost—dismissal from the court, exile, perhaps death itself—but she loved honor, loved her soul, more than life itself. That "No" made Vashti immortal, and it made Esther immortal too; for, as we shall see, had it not been for that "No" of Vashti, Esther would never have been heard of.

Esther has sodalities and societies and guilds and women named after her. But if I had a daughter I think I should like to name her Vashti.

The refusal of Vashti lost her her crown. Now a new queen, a new favorite is to be chosen. Recently there was held at Atlantic City one of those degrading beauty shows which are the shame of America. Here was the original beauty contest, not of a city, or state, or nation, but of the whole world. Every province of Ahasuerus' empire was combed for its most beautiful women, those who might be presented at the court as possible candidates for the crown of the queen of Persia. The choice fell on a young woman named Esther. Her Hebrew name was Hadassah, which means "myrtle"; but her Persian name was Esther, which means "a star." And a star Esther was, not only in physical beauty, but in beauty of soul.

This girl was a Jewess, the adopted daughter of her cousin, Mordecai, who had a post of some importance at the palace. He himself played a part in the putting forward of his lovely cousin to be the queen of Ahasuerus. So it came about that the beautiful Hebrew girl became the favorite and queen of the king of the whole earth.

Among the ministers of Ahasuerus—and now the villain of this drama—was a man named Haman. By merit he had risen to his post of prime minister. Whenever he entered or left the king's palace everyone did him reverence and bowed down—all but one man, Mordecai, who bowed not nor did him reverence. "Yet all this availeth me nothing, so long as I see Mordecai the Jew sitting at the king's gate."

Mordecai spells character. He had principles; and, like Daniel, he was true to them. His conscience forbade him to bow down and do reverence to a wicked man like Haman, and he obeyed his conscience. Without character, without loyalty to principle, man is but a beast or a clod.

Haman never forgot the insult of Mordecai, and to avenge himself he ruined his happiness, his fortune, and lost life itself. To his wife he said, after he had been honored by an invitation to the banquet with Ahasuerus and the queen, "Yet all this availeth me nothing, so long as I see Mordecai the Jew sitting at the king's gate." Here was a man who had next to the highest post in the world. From the Persian Gulf to the Caspian Sea, and from the Mediterranean to India there was not a jewel, a horse, a camel, a garment, a fruit, a woman, that Haman could not have for the asking; but all that went for nothing as long as he saw Mordecai, the Jew, refusing to do him honor. That spoiled everything for him. He forgot everything he had and centered his mind on the one thing he could not have—the reverence of Mordecai. One fly in his dish caused the whole ointment of his life to stink. But if Haman was a fool for permitting one non-bowing and dissenting Jew to ruin his happiness, he was a greater fool to permit his anger and humiliation to move him to revenge and murder.

To satisfy his hurt pride and feed his hatred Haman planned a ferocious vengeance which was to embrace the whole race of Jews to which Mordecai belonged, and in addition a particular vengeance upon Mordecai himself. Now watch the sequence of sin in Haman's heart—first pride, then revenge, then falsehood, and finally murder.

He told Ahasuerus that the nonconforming Jews scattered throughout all his kingdom were the cause of all the troubles that arose in his empire. That has a very modern sound to it. Perhaps that is where Hitler got the idea. Since it is recorded that both of them sat down to drink afterward, I think there can be little doubt that Ahasuerus was drunk when Haman got him to stamp with his signet ring the infamous edict that on the thirteenth day of the twelfth month all Jews in every province of the empire were to be put to the sword. Then Haman, at the suggestion of his wife, planned a particular revenge upon Mordecai. A gallows fifty cubits high was erected, and at the set time Haman was going to hang Mordecai on that gallows. All was ready. There could be no slip. The edict for the massacre of the Jews was signed, and there was the gallows, fifty cubits high, its rope swinging in the night wind, waiting for the neck of Mordecai. But there was Another, whom neither king nor Haman had taken into the reckoning. Behind the dim unknown God

[31]

was standing, keeping watch above his own. The gallows Haman had erected for Mordecai is going to sway the future.

The night before Mordecai was to die Ahasuerus could not sleep. Perhaps another seven-day banquet was the reason for his sleeplessness. In order to beguile the tedium of the sleepless night, Ahasuerus summoned his secretaries to read to him from the chronicles of his reign. As they read they came to a passage which related how Mordecai had saved Ahasuerus from assassination at the hands of two of his chamberlains. When the king learned that no reward had been given Mordecai for thus saving his life, he resolved to give him some signal recognition. He was debating how he should do this when there came a knock at his door. It was Haman—wicked, cruel, confident Haman—come to ask permission to hang Mordecai.

When Haman had come in, Ahasuerus, evidently suspicious now as to Haman's motives, craftily asked him, "What shall be done unto the man whom the king delighteth to honor?" "And whom," thought Haman, "could the king delight to honor more than myself?" Therefore, he suggested to the king that such a man be arrayed in royal robes, mounted on the king's Arabian charger, and conducted thus through the streets of the capital, with the man who led the horse crying out to the multitude, "Thus shall it be done to the man whom the king delighteth to honor." Then the king said, "Thou art the man! Take my horse and mount Mordecai on it, and lead him in procession through the streets."

Crestfallen and terrified, Haman did as the king commanded and led his enemy in triumph through the city. As he passed down one street he saw the gallows, fifty cubits high, which he had erected for Mordecai, the rope swinging in the morning breeze. When he saw that, there was the grip of fear at Haman's wicked heart, and he thought to himself, watching that gallows, "Mordecai the Jew got the ride on the king's horse instead of me. What if I were to get the ride on that gallows instead of Mordecai!"

That was one movement of Divine Providence— God acting through the sleepless king and the chance reading of a page from the royal chronicles. The other agency through which God acted to save Israel from annihilation was the beauty and spirit of Esther. As soon as Mordecai learned of the edict that had gone forth for the slaughter of his race, he covered himself with sackcloth and ashes and sat in mourning at the gates of the palace. Word of this was brought to the queen, who sent a messenger to Mordecai inquiring of him the reason for this act of public mourning. Then Mordecai disclosed to her the wicked plot of Haman and besought her to go to the king, Ahasuerus, and plead for the life of her people. That Esther was a Jewess had thus far been kept secret at the court. Not unnaturally, Esther feared to go into the presence of the king uncalled. That was what assassins tried to do, and whoever came into the presence of the king unsummoned was immediately put to death. Esther reminded her cousin and foster father of that law and custom. The answer of Mordecai is one of the great sayings of the Bible and of history: "For if thou altogether holdest thy peace at this time, then shall there enlargement and deliverance arise to the Jews from another place; but thou and thy father's house shall be destroyed: and who knoweth whether thou art come to the kingdom for such a time as this?"

That noble sentence struck a chord deep in Esther's breast. If it was God's will that she go in to the king, she would go. If it was God's plan to save her race through her plea before Ahasuerus, she was ready to make that plea. Asking for a fast—that is, the prayers of all Jews—Esther answered Mordecai's noble sentence with one of her own, equally noble: "So will I go in unto the king, which is not according to the law: and if I perish, I perish."

The issue of her daring and faith was that the

king extended to her the royal scepter when she came in, the sign of the royal favor, and promised to do whatever she desired.

For answer, Esther said, "Let the king and Haman come this day unto the banquet that I have prepared for him." At the banquet that night and in the presence of Haman, the king said again to Esther, "What is thy petition? . . . . and what is thy request? even to the half of the kingdom it shall be performed." But again Esther hesitates. She does not yet tell the king what her heart desires—the salvation of her people—but only requests that the king and Haman come to another banquet, which she will serve on the morrow.

Why did Esther delay to state her request? Perhaps she was hoping that there would be some happening, some event, which would strengthen her request and ensure its success. An inward voice may have told her, "Do not state your request tonight, but wait until tomorrow night." But whether Esther understood the significance of her request or not, certain it is that the hand of God was in that delay; for it was on that night—the night before the second banquet—that the king could not sleep, and learned of the service that Mordecai had rendered him in saving him from assassination, and in the caprice of his royal mind had ordered Haman to show great honor to Mordecai. Thus the mind of

[35]

the king was providentially prepared to grant the request of the beautiful queen.

On the night of the second banquet, the king again asked her her request. This time Esther did not hesitate, but said, "O king, and if it please the king, let my life be given me at my petition, and my people at my request: for we are sold, I and my people, to be destroyed, to be slain, and to perish." The amazed king, apparently forgetful of the edict he had signed, probably when he was drunk, exclaimed, "Who is he, and where is he, that durst presume in his heart to do so?" Then Esther, rising in all her majesty, and pointing to the cowering Haman, said, "The adversary and enemy is this wicked Haman." When the king heard that, he gave the order that Haman should be hanged on the gallows fifty cubits high, that he had built for Mordecai. Thus, the beauty and courage of Esther saved her race from annihilation.

PROVIDENCE IN THE LIVES OF MEN AND NATIONS

The first great truth that is brought home to us by the Book of Esther and the history of Esther is that God's purpose is being carried out in this world in the lives of men and nations, and that the plan by which God works is his divine providence. Some have been troubled about this book of the Bible because the name of God nowhere appears in its pages. Some have tried to explain this absence of the name of God from a book in God's Word on the ground that the Hebrew author of the book, living in the midst of the heathen people, found it wise to omit from his history the secret of Israel's deliverance, knowing the while that all Jews would not miss the meaning of the book. Others have claimed to find the name of God in an acrostic form in the Hebrew words. But the absence of the name of God need not trouble us. If the name of God is not there, the Fact, the Power of God, the Presence of God, is there. No book of the Bible teaches the sovereignty and the providence of God more clearly. In reality, the name of God is written on every page of the book.

And in how strange a way, and through what apparently trifling incidents the purpose of God works in the world! Here God uses the insomnia of a king and the chance reading of a page from the royal chronicles to set in motion events which saved Mordecai from death and saved Israel from death. Here we see how God works through the free and voluntary acts of men, good and bad, to carry forward his purposes. So far as Ahasuerus was concerned, it was just a chance, a happen-so, that he was unable to sleep the night before the day set for the hanging of Mordecai; and it was only a chance event again that when his secretaries read to him that night, they opened to the very page where was written the story of how Mordecai had saved him from assassination.

But what is a chance event? Is there any chance event with God? Pharaoh's daughter went down to bathe one morning in the Nile River and chanced upon that part of the river where Moses lay sleeping in his cradle in the bulrushes, and Moses was saved to deliver Israel out of the house of Egypt and the land of bondage. Columbus, nearing the American continent, turned southwest to follow the flight of birds and thus came to South America; hence North America was reserved for Anglo-Saxon and Protestant settlement. John Bunyan was drafted to stand as a sentinel when Cromwell's army was besieging an English city—probably Leicester—but at the last moment stood aside for another who had asked to serve in his place that night. The substitute was shot through the head. Bunyan lived to allure the hearts of men with his story of the Kingdom of God. So we might continue to cite apparently little incidents, to us chance events, upon which turned great events and issues. And so the lesson we learn from the pages of Esther is the lesson of Divine Providence.

In a particular sense, the story of Esther is a commentary on the history of the Jews. Haman after Haman has arisen to destroy them, but God always preserves them. Their oppressors fall and disappear. The eternal Jew goes on from age to age. God keeps his promise of old—"I will make a full end of the nations whither I have driven thee: but I will not make a full end of thee." Frederick once asked his chaplain to give him in a single sentence the proof of the existence of a God. Back came the answer: "The Jew, Your Majesty."

Faith in the providence of God gives us confidence that the affairs of this troubled world are in his hands. He never lets go of the helm of his universe. His cause is always safe. His kingdom is an everlasting kingdom. Time's drama—world rising behind world, universe behind universe—is God's drama; and here on this planet the great men, great nations, races, empires, epochs, are but the brief embodiment and transient realization of his desires.

Faith in God's providence gives us strength and confidence in our own lives. If God is present by his providence in the lives of nations, then he must also be present in the lives of individuals—and that means you and me. God's engagements in the mighty affairs of the universe do not preclude his providential direction of our own personal destiny. The book of providence, like Hebrew, must be read backward. But when we look back we can see that God was there.

GOD HAS A PLAN FOR EVERY LIFE

The other great truth taught by the history of Esther is that God has a plan for every life. When Esther awoke to that fact, she was ready for any labor and any sacrifice. It was Mordecai who brought home to her that most impressive and important fact. Until then Esther was just another beautiful Hebrew girl, basking in the pleasures of Ahasuerus' seraglio. She demurred when Mordecai asked her to go in and plead before the king for her people. She reminded him of the great risk to herself. It might cost her her life. She much preferred the warm light of the palace and the caresses of the king. But Mordecai reminded her that perhaps she had come to the throne for that very hour —"for such a time as this," for the crisis that was breaking, for the deliverance of her people from destruction. When that idea sank into the mind of Esther, it transformed her from the soft, pleasure-loving beauty, unwilling to take any risk—even for the redemption of her race—into one of the great heroines of all the ages, the woman who said, "I will go in unto the king; and if I perish, I perish."

What was true of Esther, next the throne of the master of the world, is true of the humblest daughter of Eve, true of all of us. God has a purpose in our life. For that particular purpose he has brought

[40]

us to such a place, to such a time, to such an opportunity.

This is a mighty and an encouraging truth. It warns the careless and flippant, living butterfly lives, without any serious thought or desire or purpose, that life is a serious, earnest thing. Are you living today as if God had something that he brought you into the world to do? This truth also encourages those who are cast down, depressed, or disappointed in life, who are tempted to deplore the uselessness of their lives and their labors, and wonder if God has any place for them in his great plan. Be of good courage! God not only has a place for you in the working out of his great plan, but he has a particular plan in *your* life and a particular work for *you* to do. If you are obedient to him, if you are trusting in him, if you are serving him, you are doing that work, even when you may think your life has no use or meaning.

Rise, then, to the greatness of life! Choose God's side. When Esther understood, when she saw that God was calling her to a certain work, she rose magnificently to do it, leaving behind her, still ringing down the ages, her sublime resolution, "If I perish, I perish." Paul said God has called all of us to glory and honor and immortality. Do you hear that? Do you believe that? You are called to that great destiny—honor, glory, immortality. Are you

[41]

living today as if that were true? God has sent his Son that we might have eternal life. Have you taken Christ? Have you made him your Master? Are you following him along the path that leads to that grand destiny, when, changed from glory into glory, we shall see him as he is?

III

THE WOMAN WHO WAS BETTER THAN HER JOB

> "And she bound the scarlet line in the window."
>
> JOSHUA 2:21

THIS WOMAN'S JOB WAS WHAT HAS BEEN CALLED the oldest profession; and since it is also the lowest, the least said about it the better. In one of his hymns on faith, Frederick William Faber sings:

> O gift of gifts! O grace of faith!
>   My God, how can it be
> That thou, who hast discerning love,
>   Shouldst give that gift to me?
>
> How many hearts thou mightst have had
>   More innocent than mine,
> How many souls more worthy far
>   Of that sweet touch of thine!
>
> Ah, grace, into unlikeliest hearts
>   It is thy boast to come;
> The glory of thy light to find
>   In darkest spots a home.

When Rahab believed and was saved, that was the very song she might have sung, had it then been written, for, in truth, that was what happened in her case. She might well have wondered that God, who has discerning love, should have given that gift to her. She must have thought of the many hearts in Jericho which were far more worthy of that sweet touch of God's Holy Spirit.

To humble our pride and to teach us that we are saved by the grace of God, God took a harlot and by her teaches us the meaning of faith.

Climb with me now to this mountaintop on the other side the Jordan River. Israel's great leader, Moses, has finished his work. On Nebo's lonely mountain, in a vale in the land of Moab, Moses slept in his unknown grave. But before Moses died he laid his hands upon that valiant soldier, Joshua, and appointed him his successor. Moses had led the people out of Egypt, through the wanderings of the forty years in the burning deserts, and had brought them to the river Jordan, in the land of Moab. But to Joshua fell the dangerous and diffi-cult task of taking the people over the river and con-quering the land of Canaan.

Like a wise soldier and general, before he crosses the river and attacks Jericho Joshua makes a recon-naissance. There he stands on the top of the moun-tain looking off toward the land of Canaan. Far below him lies the encampment of Israel. In the center is the Tabernacle with the Ark of the Covenant. About the Tabernacle are encamped the twelve tribes of Israel—Levi, Judah, Simeon, Benjamin, Dan, Issachar, and the rest of them—their standards waving in the spring sunshine. Beyond the encampment flows the Jordan River, swollen with the spring rains and "overflowing all his banks." Across the river lay the land of Canaan, forever now the Holy Land. There it lay; the land of Israel's future history, the stage of divine redemption; the land forever to be associated with Israel's patriarchs and kings and captains, prophets and apostles; with Israel's conquests, apostasies, exiles, and restorations; with her temple worship; and with the fulfillment of the grand hopes and prophecies of God's people—the incarnation, the miracles, the crucifixion, the resurrection, the ascension into heaven, the outpouring of the Holy Spirit, and the beginning of the Christian church.

Beyond the river Joshua saw the fertile plain of the Jordan valley; to the north the Sea of Galilee, and to the south the Dead Sea. Yonder is Jericho with her thick walls and towering ramparts; and yonder the mountain eminence, the Jebusite stronghold, which will be known and forever venerated by mankind as Jerusalem. To the south of that mount lies Bethlehem, where Christ will be born; and far in the distance Joshua can see the gleam and flash of the Great Sea itself. This was the "goodly land" he was to conquer.

Calling to him two soldiers of proven courage and character, Joshua points out to them the stronghold of Jericho, directly across the river, and tells them he wants them to explore the city. They are to bring him a report of its walls and gates, its state of preparation, the number of its inhabitants, the size of its army. "Go view the land, even Jericho." It was a difficult and dangerous assignment. But that evening, when night had come down, the two men set forth. An interesting tradition has it that Salmon, who afterward married Rahab, was one of the spies. If so, this finishing touch of romance makes the story of Rahab one of the most fascinating in the Bible. First they crossed the flooded Jordan and then made their way, probably in the disguise of merchants, to Jericho, where they passed through the gates of the city, and, asking for the house of a harlot—for merchants frequently made such houses their stopping places—were directed to the home of Rahab.

In spite of their disguise, the presence of the two strangers in Jericho at once aroused suspicion, especially in view of the common knowledge of the near approach of the host of Israel. Officers of the king watched where the two men went and at once reported their whereabouts to their master. The king immediately dispatched soldiers to take them. When the soldiers came to Rahab's door, they said to her, "Bring forth the men that are come to thee, which are entered into thine house: for they be come to search out all the country."

But instead of producing the strangers, Rahab hid them and protected them. She immediately discerned that these two men were different from others who had come to her home. They were perhaps the first who had not entered it for the purposes of sin. The Spirit of God, unaided, could have produced in the harlot's heart the impression that these men represented God and his cause, and therefore must not be molested; but it is more likely that, as he often does, the Holy Spirit worked that night through human agents. These men spoke to Rahab of the God of Israel, and of the great destiny of the people of God. What they told her reached her heart, and she believed the spies. Rahab must have felt that her great hour had struck, and that it was her God-appointed destiny to hide the spies and to help the people of Israel and serve the God of Israel.

Since these men represented God's holy cause, she determined to protect and save them from the wrath of the king of Jericho. So a harlot became God's servant and messenger when the soldiers came pounding on her door. She told them that two men— whence, she knew not—had come to her house that day; but about the time for the shutting of the gates of the city they had gone their way—whither, she knew not. "But," she said to the soldiers, "it is such a short time since they departed that you will have no trouble in coming up with them if you pursue hastily." Supposing that the two men had taken the road back to the fords of the Jordan, the soldiers hurried off in that direction.

It was a vain chase; for all the time the spies of Joshua were hiding on the roof of Rahab's house, where, upon the first appearance of the soldiers to inquire after them, she had hid them under the stalks of flax which were drying there. Like Lydia, the purple seller of Thyatira, who became the first convert to Christianity in Europe when Paul preached at Philippi, Rahab, the first convert to Judaism from the heathen world, seems to have been a dyer and a seller of linen, as well as a harlot.

As soon as the soldiers were out of hearing, Rahab went up to the housetop. A great wave of penitence, of yearning for a higher life, and a thirst after God, undoubtedly filled the heart of Rahab that night. There, on the roof of the house, in the silence of the night, with the stars looking down upon the heathen city which lay all quiet about her, and the grim mountains rising in the distance, their harshness softened in the evening shadows, Rahab made to the spies her great confession of faith. She told them she knew that God had given the city and the land to Israel, for she had heard of their mighty conquests on the way up from Egypt. There were other gods, the cruel and licentious gods of Jericho and Canaan; but she was convinced, she said, that the only true God was the God of Israel. "For the Lord your God, he is God in heaven above, and in earth beneath."

The spies had come to investigate the strength of Jericho and its mighty walls, reports concerning which had reached Joshua and his army. But that night they listened to earnest words from the erstwhile heathen lips of a woman who tells them how strong God is in Israel. So the heathen harlot strengthens the faith of the Hebrew spies in their own God! When Gideon still feared to attack the host of Midian with his army of three hundred men, God told him to go down that night into the host of Midian, and "thou shalt hear what they say." That night, listening against one of the black tents of the Midianites, Gideon heard one of them relate his dream to his fellow—the dream of the barley loaf that came tumbling down and knocked over the tent. The interpretation given that dream was that God would deliver Midian into the hands of Gideon. Thus strengthened, Gideon went back and led his army to its great victory. Yes, "thou shalt hear what they say!" Often in the camp of unbelief, in the world which appears so hostile to the church, there are spoken secret appraisals of the strength and the influence of the church, of Christ, his Cross and the godly life, which, if we could listen to them, would hearten us and strengthen our faith.

Considering the time, the place, the hour, the circumstances, and that it was a harlot who made it, this is one of the most remarkable confessions of faith in the Bible. And it is not strange that, ages after, the faith that inspired it is spoken of along with that of Abraham and Moses and Enoch and Noah.

Her first request is not for herself, but for her father's house. Like all noble souls she was concerned for the welfare of others. Rahab did not care to be saved alone. In return for her kindness to the spies she begs that they will show kindness to her father's house, and asks that they seal their promise with a sign and token. The spies assured her that if she followed their directions her life and the lives of all her father's household would be saved. Then Rahab took one of the scarlet ropes which she had dyed and which she used in her business, and binding it about the waist of one of the spies, lowered him from the window to the ground below. The rope was released by the first spy and drawn up again to the window by Rahab, who quickly bound it about the waist of the second spy, and in the same manner lowered him safely to the ground. This was in order that they would not have to pass out of the gate of the city and thus risk capture and death.

Then the two men called up to Rahab to bind the rope to the window, letting it hang down over the wall, and when the city was attacked by Joshua's army, his soldiers, informed in advance, would spare her house and all her people when they saw that scarlet rope floating from the window.

Then the two men departed, and at the wise advice of Rahab, instead of starting back at once toward the Jordan, went into the mountains west of Jericho. There they lay hid for three days, and then retraced their steps across the Jordan to make their report to Joshua. When Joshua heard the remarkable story of Rahab, he felt sure that God would give him the victory in the coming battle. "Truly the Lord hath delivered into our hands all the land."

As soon as the sun was up the next morning, Rahab hurried through the streets to the home of her father and mother. It may have been that she had never crossed the threshold of that home since she took up her sinful calling, and we can imagine the joy and surprise of the father and mother when they saw their long-lost daughter return. But it was not a time for rejoicing. Rahab said to them:

"Come with me! The army of the Israelites, led by Jehovah, will surely take and destroy Jericho and all its people; but I have secured a promise from the Hebrew spies, whom I hid from the king's soldiers, that if I hang the scarlet thread from the window of my house they will spare me and all my family. Come with me!" And all her kindred who believed her word followed her back through the streets and took refuge in her house, high up on the wall of the city.

When, after the miraculous crossing of the Jordan, the army of Israel moved against Jericho, Joshua gave strict orders that in the general destruction of the city and its inhabitants Rahab and all her household were to be spared, because she had hid the spies and confessed her faith in the God of Israel. For six days the people, in ominous silence, save for the blast of the priests on the rams' horns, marched around the prodigious walls of Jericho, while the defenders looked down and jeered from the ramparts of the city.

As Joshua's army encircled the city on those successive days, I can see Rahab standing at the window, watching the army as it marches past, and back of her her father and mother, her brothers and sisters, and all her kindred. The spies, too, were in that army, and perhaps they waved a greeting to Rahab when they saw her standing at the window where the scarlet cord was floating in the breeze.

On the seventh day they encircled the city seven times; and when, on the seventh round, the priests sounded with their horns, the walls of Jericho fell flat and the army of Joshua rushed into the doomed city with drawn swords. The fearful work of vengeance and destruction was complete. But through the carnage and the debris and the dust of fallen structures, the two spies made their way quickly in the direction of the house of Rahab. There they saw streaming from the window the red cord which Rahab, faithful to their directions, had hung there. Entering into the house and going up to the chamber on the wall, the spies tied the rope about Rahab and lowered her to a place of safety amid the army of Israel. Then her father and mother and all her kindred were lowered to safety in the same way. The same scarlet rope that had saved the spies saved Rahab. Ever afterward she dwelt with the people of Israel; and if in the table of our Lord's ancestors in Matthew's Gospel [1] Rachab, the wife of Salmon, the mother of Boaz, means Rahab, then Rahab the harlot had the high honor of being one of our Lord's ancestors. That, in brief, is the story of Rahab the harlot, the woman who was better than her job.

[1] Matthew 1:5.

BEAUTY IN STRANGE PLACES

The history of Rahab is, in the first place, a striking illustration of the fact that beauty of character and Christian faith may be planted of God in most unlikely places. There must have been hundreds of virtuous women in Jericho then, but all were passed over by the electing grace of God for a harlot. Rahab was capable of a faith that receives mention from age to age.

That was something that our Lord himself liked to emphasize and show—the beautiful possibilities of a soul even in the lowest state. So he said that publicans and harlots would go into the kingdom of heaven before many self-righteous persons who thought they had no need of salvation. Rahab's story is a tribute to the possibilities of every human soul. The woman who was a sinner lives forever in Christian memory, for Christ found a place in her darkest heart. The masters of human thought and fiction have liked to dwell upon this high capacity of the most unlikely lives. Among instances we think of are Quasimodo in Victor Hugo's *Notre-Dame,* and Miriam in Charles Kingsley's *Hypatia.* Kingsley thus eloquently describes the better woman in the heart of that witch and panderer:

Her grim, withered features grew softer, purer, grander, and rose ennobled for a moment to their long-lost might-have-been, to that personal ideal which every soul brings with it into the world, which shines dim and potential in the face of every sleeping babe, before it has been scarred and distorted and incrusted in the long tragedy of life. Sorceress she was, panderer and slave dealer, steeped to the lips in falsehood, ferocity, and avarice, yet that paltry stone brought home to her some thought, true, spiritual, impalpable, unmarketable, before which all her treasures and all her ambitions were as worthless in her own eyes as they were in the eyes of the angels of God.

THE POWER OF DECISION FOR GOD

Again, in the history of Rahab we see the importance and the power of decision for God. In the divine goodness of God, the knowledge of the true God and the way of life was presented to her by those spies who had come to her house. Rahab was not only convinced, but *acted* upon her convictions and chose the destiny of the people of God. She was not only impressed, but *acted* at once upon her impressions; disregarding the personal risk involved, she hid and protected the two spies, and then made her confession of faith and her irrevocable decision. Where a firm decision for God is made in a human life, there the foundation of all future success and strength is laid; but where there is no firm decision, no matter what earnest and deep impressions and desires there may be, the fruits of the Christian life will never make their appearance. Balaam, like Rahab, knew that God was with the Israelites. He was impressed with their future destiny and desired to share in that destiny. When he was hired by the kings of Moab to curse the invaders, instead of cursing them he blessed them in terms of incomparable eloquence, and made his celebrated prayer, "Let me die the death of the righteous, and let my last end be like his." But his longing was not followed by decision and choice. Unlike Rahab, he was not willing to pay the price, and, lured by the gold of Moab, instead of dying the death of a servant of God, he died miserably in battle against the people of God. Your feelings may be all right; but without decision and choice those feelings will be as vain as the summer wind. You believe in God, in Christ, in his atonement on the cross, in the heavenly life to come. But does your life show that by your daily confession? Have you separated yourself from the world, as Rahab separated herself from the people of Jericho and chose the people of God?

SAVING FAITH

But the thing about Rahab which the Bible emphasizes—and it always emphasizes the great thing—is her faith. In that grand roll call of the heroes and heroines of faith in the eleventh chapter of the Letter to the Hebrews the name of Rahab the harlot is forever inscribed. "By faith the harlot Rahab perished not with them that believed not, when she had received the spies with peace."

What were the characteristics of the faith of Rahab that make it worthy of such high mention? It was faith where all others believed not. All the other inhabitants of Jericho must have jeered and scoffed at Joshua's army, when it marched around the walls of the heathen stronghold. Only Rahab looked upon that army in faith and believed that God was with it. It was faith that counted all else to be loss save that in which she put her faith. It was faith that showed itself by works, without which our faith is dead. She believed in God and in the destiny of the people of God; and she matched her faith by her works, for she hid and protected the spies. James does not contradict the statement of the Hebrews or the statement of Paul that Rahab was saved by faith, when he asks "Likewise also was not Rahab the harlot justified by works, when she had received the messengers, and had sent them out another way?" You believe in God; you trust in Christ; you accept the glorious destiny of the redeemed. But do you back that faith up by your works, by your daily life?

THE SCARLET CORD AND THE BLOOD OF CHRIST

It is not strange that in that scarlet cord waving from the window of Rahab's house on Jericho's wall when the city was being destroyed by the army of Joshua, and which saved her and her household, Christian faith should have seen a symbol of the saving power of the Cross of Christ, and faith in that Cross. How could a waving scarlet cord save Rahab's house from the doom of Jericho? There was certainly nothing in the situation of Rahab's house which guaranteed its safety, for it stood high up on the wall, in the most dangerous place of all. How could a scarlet thread save that house? Yet it did. How can our faith in the Cross of Christ, that scarlet cord of mercy which God has flung out from the windows of heaven, save us from death and reconcile us to God and bless our lives with unending joy and happiness hereafter? Yet that is the promise of the Word of God. Have you taken God at his word when he says, "He that believeth . . . . shall be saved"? Is the scarlet thread of the Cross, of Christ's blood, over your soul? Is it over your home and your household? Are you concerned for that household as Rahab was for hers? I can show you the spot in our old home where our mother offered her daily prayers for her children. Can you mothers show me the spot in your home where you pray for your children? Will they be able to go back to the old home—your children—and say, "There mother prayed for me"? Is the scarlet thread of your faith in the redeeming blood of Christ waving in the window of your soul? God has made his eternal promise that he that believeth in the Lord Jesus Christ shall be saved. He will keep that promise as faithfully as Joshua did when he destroyed Jericho, but spared the house of Rahab the harlot, where the scarlet cord was waving. Is the cord there today? Are you trusting in the Cross? One day the trumpets of judgment will sound, as they sounded of old over ancient and doomed Jericho. But where the scarlet cord waves, there is safety and refuge. "The blood of Jesus Christ his Son cleanseth us from all sin."

IV

THE WOMAN TO REMEMBER

"But his wife looked back from behind
him, and she became a pillar of salt."

.GENESIS 19:26

OUR LORD IN HIS TEACHING AND PREACHING
handed down to immortality of fame two women.
One was that woman who anointed his head and
feet with costly ointment and dried his feet with
the hair of her head. Of that woman Jesus said
that wherever his Gospel should be preached
throughout the whole world what she had done
would be spoken of as a memorial of her. And
that has come to pass. Again today, in a part of
the world not then known to be in existence, the
name of that woman is mentioned.

The other was Lot's wife, who turned back and
became a pillar of salt. In the midst of one of
his sermons, when he was speaking of the separations
and sacrifices which true religion requires of the
soul, Jesus suddenly uttered that solemn warning,
"Remember Lot's wife." It is Christ himself, then,
who, among all the women of the Old Testament,
singles out Lot's wife as one whose fate is to be

studied and remembered by every Christian who is in earnest about the salvation of his soul.

That is all that is told us of Lot's wife, that she looked back and became a pillar of salt, and that Christ made use of her doom to illustrate his sermon. But that is enough. All the rest it is not difficult to fill in. Lot's wife looked back because the world she had come to love was in Sodom. There was her treasure, and there her heart also.

Let us review a little of the history of Lot and his family before this event, when his wife perished as Sodom was burning. Lot was the nephew of Abraham. His herdsmen had fought with the herdsmen of Abraham over places of pasturage. Instead of backing up his herdsmen and continuing the quarrel, Abraham suggested that he and Lot and their followers and flocks should separate, each choosing a section of the country as his dwelling place. With characteristic generosity, Abraham gave Lot the first choice. Lot saw that the most fertile part of the country was the valley of the Jordan. He must have known that it bordered the wicked cities of Sodom and Gomorrah, but he no doubt felt that he could take care of himself and keep his family uncontaminated by the wickedness of those cities. Therefore he chose the land toward the south and pitched his tent toward Sodom.

Mark that! He pitched his tent toward Sodom.

He did not take up his abode in Sodom, neither did he settle down close to its walls; but he pitched his tent toward Sodom. That was the section where he chose his territory, and that was the general direction in which his encampment looked. There are a lot of people who are not yet in the Sodom of wickedness and denial of God. Their names are not yet inscribed on the roll of the citizens of that place. But there is a certain set of the sails of their life, a certain tone and color and inclination—a pitch of their tent, which is in the direction of Sodom. What about you? Are you pitching your tent toward Sodom? Are you going along with the world rather than with the church? Are you inclining more to the people of Sodom than to the people of God? Then take heed lest you become a full-fledged citizen of Sodom. That was what happened to Lot and his wife.

The cup of Sodom's iniquity was now full to overflowing. "Wheresoever the carcass is," said Christ, "there will the eagles be gathered together." There is a "thus far and no farther" with God, and when men or nations cross that line, then come the vultures of judgment and retribution. When the angels told Abraham of the approaching doom of Sodom and Gomorrah, he pleaded with God to spare the cities, and got from God the promise that if Sodom could muster ten righteous men he would not destroy the city. But that many, or that few, righteous men could not be found in the place, and God looses the thunderbolts of his wrath and judgment.

LOST INFLUENCE

The one righteous man, however, that there was in Sodom, and his family, received a warning in time to be saved. When Lot learned the coming doom of the city he at once went to speak to his sons-in-law, and said to them, "Up, get you out of this place; for the Lord will destroy this city." But Lot had lived too long in Sodom to be taken seriously. His sons-in-law thought he was joking. "He seemed to them as one that mocked." And just before that, when Lot had rebuked the men of Sodom for the terrible and shameful proposal they made concerning the angels who had come to warn him—a fearful sin which has taken its name from Sodom—they said one to another, "This one fellow came in to sojourn, and he will needs be a judge!" What they meant was, "Who is this Lot, who dwells in Sodom, has chosen it for his abode, and now preaches morality to us!" Thus Lot had lost his influence, both with his sons-in-law and with the citizens of Sodom. When he wishes to be taken seriously, they think he is mocking. He seemed to them as one that mocked! What is sadder than the passing of influence? And how easily it passes. The wrong kind of a glance, the wrong kind of a word, the little mean advantage, the lack of earnestness or sincerity, a little departure from the truth, and our power to influence some immortal soul for eternal life is ruined and lost. We seem to them as one that mocks.

WHEN DEATH STRIKES

All Lot could persuade to leave the city with him were his wife and his two daughters. Imagination staggers when we try to envisage the doom that fell upon those towns. At Pompeii the visitor looks upon the lava-encased bodies of those who perished in that great eruption of Vesuvius, and gets some idea of the terrors of that disaster and judgment. There they lie, just as they were, and at the very work in which they were engaged when the fiery flood overflowed them. So it must have been at Sodom and Gomorrah. The peasant was plowing with the oxen in the fields near the city; the baker was at work before his oven; the priest was ministering in the temple before his idols; the merchant was counting his money and taking an inventory of his goods; the housewife was busy in the kitchen; the scribe was writing with his pen; the rich man was driving by in his chariot; the beggar had his hand out for an alms; the thief, the drunkard, and the adulterer were in the midst of their sins, when death overtook them. An appalling disaster and judgment. And yet, was there anything singular about that? Is not that the way death always comes? It stops men in their tracks. It stops the preacher in his pulpit, the scholar in his study, the soldier in his battle, the lover in his embrace, the singer in his music, the plowman in his furrow, the good man in his good work, and the wicked man in his deed of wickedness. Just as we are, death takes us. Then there can be no change, no alteration, and what we have written we have written. Let us live, then, in the light of this truth, and be ready for the touch of that hand which, so far as this world and its opportunities, its hopes, its sorrows, its disappointments, its ambitions, its transgressions, and its fears are concerned, arrests and stops us forever.

A FATAL LOOK

The angels who took Lot and his wife by the hand and led them out of the city said to him, "Escape for thy life; look not behind thee, neither stay thou in all the plain; escape to the mountain, lest thou be consumed." But as they journeyed toward the mountain, Lot's wife, disregarding the injunction of the angels, stopped and, turning, looked toward the doomed cities. That moment she became a pillar of salt.

The fate of Lot's wife has an interesting counter·

part, although altogether different in the lesson which it teaches, in the ancient myth of Orpheus. Orpheus was the most famous musician of his day, and when he played upon his lyre not only his fellow mortals but even wild animals were softened and subdued by his melodious strains. The very trees and rocks were sensible to the charm of his music. When his wife Eurydice, fleeing from the shepherd Aristaeus, was bitten in the foot by a snake and died, Orpheus resolved to seek his wife in the regions of the dead. With his lyre he went through the realms of Pluto, and sang in such tender and mournful strains that even the very ghosts shed tears. Tantalus ceased for a moment in his efforts for water. Ixion's wheel stood still. The daughters of Danaus rested from their task of drawing water in a sieve, and Sisyphus sat on his rock to listen. It was the greatest triumph of music ever recorded. Pluto at length gave his consent for Eurydice to return with Orpheus to the upper air, but upon condition that he should not turn round and look upon her until they had emerged from Hades. Through all the horrors of hell they passed safely, and were on the very verge of the light of the upper air when Orpheus, "unmindful of fate, alas! and soul subdued, look back." That moment Eurydice became a ghost again. So a soul's happiness may be lost by one backward glance.

Lot's wife was *almost* saved; yet she was lost because she looked back. We speak of her as a "social-ite who became salt," because in many ways she is a type of those women, and men too, who start on the Christian life, accept in general the great truths of Christianity, but, because their hearts have never been changed, go back and perish.

THE HEART AND ITS TREASURE

Lot's wife's heart was in Sodom because her treasure was there. When Lot moved into Sodom, I have no doubt it was at the urging of his wife. The life in the city appealed to her far more than the roving existence in the black tents, with the smell of sheep and goats and camels always about her. In the city she became a fine lady, lived in a mansion on Main Street, met with the other select women in their homes, was pointed out as Lot's wife. It was not strange that she did not want to forsake Sodom and all its pleasures.

When Lot first made the announcement that they must get out of the city, his wife, I suppose, plagued him to stay. She pointed to the sky, asking Lot to show where there was even the smallest cloud to indicate the coming storm. Why be upset by the word of two men he had never seen before? Probably it was a scheme to get him out of the city so that others might seize his property. "This fine house, Lot—do you want me to leave it for one of those black tents and become a wandering Bedouin again? Why should I give up my comforts here, all my costly, fashionable gowns, and the friends I have made here? And there are our daughters. Their husbands will not go with them. They know only the city life, and they are just getting into the higher social circles of Sodom."

HALFWAY CHRISTIANS

Yet, despite her protests, Lot persuaded her to accompany him from the city. In that respect she is like many others who come into the church and start the Christian life, but half unwillingly, and with no joy or conviction or desire. Some distance from the city, Lot's wife again, I suppose, besieged him with her complaints and voiced her desire to go back. But Lot reminded her of what the angels had said and urged her to go on. On, then, with heavy, dragging feet, she went. As a rule it is the husband who is a dead weight on the spiritual life of the wife, but here it is the wife who tries to hold her husband back. Among the saddest experiences of the minister are those homes where a wife holds back a husband in his religious life, keeps him from church, and, unless he has sufficient independence and courage, will keep him out of the Kingdom of Heaven. That, I say, is one of the saddest spectacles that the minister ever beholds. And whenever he sees it he thinks of Lot's wife. So far as turning back and looking back were concerned, Lot's wife might just as well do so, for her heart had already looked back —and out of the heart are the issues of life.

THE NEW BIRTH

Thus we come back to that fundamental necessity of every true Christian life—the new birth. It is as essential to spiritual life as physical birth is to physical life. "Except a man be born again," said the Author of all spiritual life, "he cannot see the kingdom of God." But when we say a man *must* be born again, we never say it without also saying a man *can* be born again, a woman *can* be born again. That is the glorious possibility for us all.

ONLY ONE LOOK!

It was just one look that Lot's wife took, and yet by that one look she became a pillar of salt. In a moment of time, in the yielding or acquiescence of a single second, irreparable injury can be done to the soul. Only one look from his palace roof at a woman bathing on the roof of another house, and King David—God-loving, psalm-singing David, he who strikes every chord in the heart of man—went staggering and reeling and plunging down into the abyss of his sin. Who can measure the possibilities for good or evil in a moment of time? In a moment of time the devil showed Christ the kingdoms of this world and their glory, and asked for his worship; and in that same moment of time Christ won the victory and said, "Get thee behind me, Satan."

If by only one look, if in only one moment of time, a deep injury can be wrought to the soul, it is equally true that in the resistance of a moment of time, in the choice of a moment of time, in the earnest heartfelt prayer of a moment of time, temptation can be conquered and eternal life secured. How eloquent, and also how moving and pathetic, was that last prayer of blind Samson, as they led him forth to make sport for the Philistines in the temple of Dagon. "O Lord God, remember me, I pray thee, and strengthen me, I pray thee, *only this once.*" By an "only this once"—one foolish yielding to the blandishments of the lovely siren Delilah—Samson had been cast into slavery and blindness. Now he asked God to remember him, "only this once." That prayer was granted, and by one final great exploit for God the past transgressions of Samson were atoned.

WHEN ANGELS TAKE US BY THE HAND

Lot's wife had many advantages, yet she was lost. She had a godly husband, still uncontaminated by the society of Sodom, yet she was lost. She had the memories of her association with godly Abraham, yet she was lost. She had the warning of the angels and the pleading of her husband, yet she was lost. She had too the special intervention of the angels. They took her and her husband by the hand. Yes, angels took her by the hand. Yet Lot's wife was lost.

Lot's wife was not the only woman, not the only person, whom angels have taken by the hand. I invoke now to your memory and your conscience some of those angels who have taken you by the hand: the memory of a godly father, of a praying mother, who never once looked back on her heavenward journey; the sense, the feeling of the emptiness, the nothingness of much that this world holds and pursues; the sorrow that came over you when a loved one of your circle was laid in the grave; the pangs that conscience inflicted upon you when you sinned; the sigh and longing for a better life that once escaped your heart and your lips; the weariness or weakness of the flesh that intimated to you that your strength was not forever, and that ere long you too must go the way of all the earth; the moving of the heart as you listened to sermon, song, or prayer that spoke of Christ's undying love for sinners. What are these but God's angels taking you by the hand to lead you from the city of danger and death to the City of Life? Yes! angels of Jesus are they; angels of light, seeking to bring the pilgrim safe home to heaven. May those angels not take us by the hand in vain! Come, holy, compassionate angels! Take us by the hand and lead us out of the plains of sin and danger to the high tablelands of peace and safety. Lead us from our follies, our waywardness, our transgressions, into the presence of God, our Father!

V

THE WOMAN WHO COOKED AND THE WOMAN WHO PRAYED

"And Martha served."

JOHN 12:2

"Mary, which also sat at Jesus' feet."

LUKE 10:39

THESE TWO SISTERS APPEAR IN THREE UNFORGET-table scenes in the Gospels, and the artists who sketch them for us are Luke and John. Luke sketches them in the first and opening scene, and John in the two other scenes. The first scene, shows the sisters at a supper with our Lord; the second shows them at a funeral; and the third at a banquet. But in every scene they appear with the same unmistakable characteristics. One is the busy efficient woman who cooks and serves; the other is the woman who sits at Jesus' feet, the woman who prays.

As you go out from Jerusalem, taking the road to Jericho, you come to Bethany—about three miles along the road, just where it begins to drop down toward Jericho. In this village lived Lazarus with his two sisters, Martha and Mary. Martha seems to have been the head of the house, for Luke tells us that "a certain woman named Martha received him into her house." Some have conjectured that she was the widow of Simon the Leper, for Matthew states that it was in Simon's house that the banquet celebrating the resurrection of Lazarus was held. We do not know how the relationship between this family and Jesus was established. Perhaps Martha in her grief after the death of her husband had gone to Jesus. Perhaps—and more likely—on one of his journeys Jesus stopped one day at their door in Bethany and asked for a drink of water. But however established, the friendship was beautiful and mutually profitable. Jesus once said that the foxes had holes and the birds of the air had nests, but the Son of Man had not where to lay his head. So far as ownership was concerned, that was true; but it is a satisfaction to recall that there were at least two homes where the Son of Man was always a welcomed and beloved guest. One was the home of Peter at Capernaum; the other was this home at Bethany. Who can tell what that home meant to Jesus? There always awaited him a warm welcome, tender kindness, true sympathy, and deep understanding. All we know of the brother in the house, aside from his death and resurrection, is that Jesus loved him and wept over him when he was dead. It was a home where love reigned; and without love what is home?

Oft Jesus on his journeys of mercy and teaching stopped at this Bethany home and was refreshed; and it was that home, Matthew tells us, that was his refuge and resting place in the week of his passion and death. I imagine that Bethany home was to Jesus what the home of the Shunammite woman with its prophet's chamber was to Elisha as he made his journeys up and down the land. I imagine it was to Jesus what the home of Sir Thomas Abney was for thirty-six years to Isaac Watts. I imagine that home of Bethany was to Jesus what the home of Mary Unwin was to William Cowper, the great poet and hymn writer. In her home Cowper lived for nineteen years; and in one of his noblest sonnets he commemorated the love and care of Mary Unwin:

Mary! I want a lyre with other strings;
Such aid from Heaven as some have feigned they drew!
An eloquence scarce given to mortals, new,
And undebased by praise of meaner things!
That, ere through age or woe I shed my wings,
I may record thy worth, with honour due,
In verse as musical as thou art true,—
Verse that immortalises whom it sings!
But thou hast little need: there is a book,
By seraphs writ with beams of heavenly light,
On which the eyes of God not rarely look;
A chronicle of actions just and bright!
    There all thy deeds, my faithful Mary, shine,
    And since thou own'st that praise, I spare thee mine.

SCENE I: A SUPPER

Let us look now at these two sisters; first in the

supper scene which is related by Luke. "Now it came to pass, as they went, that he entered into a certain village; and a certain woman named Martha received him into her house." Jesus was traveling through the country with his disciples, perhaps coming up from Jericho; for he had just related the story of the Good Samaritan, who showed kindness to a man beaten and robbed on that road. No doubt, Jesus sent a messenger ahead to inform the friends at Bethany that they could expect him for supper that night. His disciples, of course, were included among the visitors; and we can see Martha, when she received word of the approach of that considerable company, going energetically to work to prepare for the loved guest and his friends.

One servant is dispatched to the market for food, and others are directed to get the guestchamber ready. In the midst of the bustle of preparation Jesus arrives. After the first Oriental kiss of welcome and the washing of the feet, Jesus sits down to rest in the cool shade of the courtyard, where the vines are clambering over the walls. There Mary joins him, while Martha hurries off to direct the servants and prepare the repast. It was no slight task to prepare for so many, and Martha is somewhat anxious and heated as she helps the servants in the hot kitchen and prepares the table.

In the midst of her exertions she bethinks herself

of Mary. "Where is Mary? Why doesn't she help me with the work?" Off she goes to search for her, and finds her in the cool courtyard sitting at the feet of Jesus, looking raptly and fondly into his face and drinking in his words of wisdom. For the moment Martha loses her temper, and exclaims to Jesus, "Lord, dost thou not care that my sister hath left me to serve alone? bid her therefore that she help me." Jesus answers this rude intrusion and interruption in calm, patient words, saying to Martha, "Martha, Martha, thou art careful and troubled about many things: but one thing is needful: and Mary hath chosen that good part, which shall not be taken away from her."

Jesus did not rebuke Martha for her zeal and industry. Somebody had to prepare the supper; and if Martha, too, had spent all her time sitting at the feet of Jesus, he and the disciples would have gone hungry that night. God bless all thoughtful, busy, efficient housekeepers like Martha. A young man looking for a wife would do well to ascertain if the one he looks upon with favor has some of the qualities of Martha. Martha's housekeeping qualities will wear much longer than rouged beauty, enameled nails, and permanent waves. The divorce records would be cut down considerably if more wives had a little more of Martha in them.

But it is clear from the words of Jesus to Martha

[77]

that she was in danger of putting too great emphasis on the practical, busy side of life, to the neglect of the devotional and contemplative side. The ideal woman would combine the practical and the devotional; but the devotional can be omitted only to the hurt of the soul. There is too little quietness and meditation and prayer in the world today, and too little of it among our women, many of whom are stirring about in their divers clubs and organizations, commendably busy and cumbered with care of the social welfare of the community, but somewhat to the neglect of worship and prayer. All the old-time Christian homes used to have in them works of devotion and meditation which were read and pondered. Today those books have almost disappeared. Even the one great book of devotion, the Bible, gets little attention in the ordinary home.

What about you, my friend? Are you cumbered with the cares of this world? Are you giving more thought to them than to the spiritual needs of your soul? If so, hear those words of Jesus to Martha: "Thou art careful and troubled about many things: but one thing is needful: and Mary hath chosen that good part, which shall not be taken away from her." No! Time and fate will take away from you all those things about you with which you have been so busy. One by one they pass and disappear; but the "good part," your relationship to Christ your Re-

deemer, the care which you bestow upon your soul
—that abides forever.

An old legend relates that once on a cold stormy
night Martha was busy in her home preparing for
the expected Christ. In the midst of her preparations
there was a gentle knock on the door. Opening the
door, Martha saw a ragged beggar standing there in
the wet and cold. Immediately she shut the door on
the beggar, saying, as she did so, "I am expecting
Jesus, the great prophet of Galilee, tonight. I have
no time for beggars. Come again." After a little
there was another gentle knock on the door. This
time, when Martha opened the door she saw a frail,
ill child standing without. To this child also Martha
said, "I am expecting Jesus tonight. I have no time
to give to you." But before she could close the door,
suddenly Jesus, in all his majesty, stood before her!
Martha had been too busy to recognize her Lord.
How is it with you? Are you so busy that you cannot recognize Christ when he comes? Are you so
engaged with the world that you cannot recognize
and hear the voice of God when he speaks to your
soul?

SCENE II : A FUNERAL

The next scene is also at Bethany; but it is not a
banquet this time, but the house of sorrow. Lazarus,
whom Jesus loved, lay dead and buried. When his

sickness had become serious, the sisters sent word to Jesus, who was across the Jordan, saying, "He whom thou lovest is sick." They thought that would bring him at once. But the hours and the days slipped by, and Jesus did not come. But death came, as it will come to all. Finally, Jesus also came. The house at Bethany was filled with friends of the family, who had come to show their sympathy by wailing. When word came that Jesus was at hand, Martha arose and ran to meet him, crying out, with gentle expostulation, "Lord, if thou hadst been here, my brother had not died." But that was immediately followed by one of the most beautiful confessions of faith in Christ that mortal lips ever expressed: "But I know, that even now, whatsoever thou wilt ask of God, God will give it thee." There we have the ground of Christian prayer. We pray in the Name of Christ; and God will do great things for Christ's sake.

Then Jesus spoke to Martha about the resurrection. When Martha replied that she knew her brother would rise at the last day, Jesus answered with his great grave-shaking affirmation, "I am the resurrection, and the life!" Awed by that utterance, Martha returned to the house, and going to the room where Mary was weeping by herself, said to her, "The Master is come, and calleth for thee." When Mary heard that, she hurried to meet Jesus and fell down at his feet, saying just what Martha had said before her: "Lord, if thou hadst been here, my brother had not died." When Jesus saw her weeping, and heard the Jews weeping, he himself wept. There you have it—the shortest, and in some ways the greatest, sentence of the Gospels: "Jesus Wept." Then followed the great scene at the sepulcher when Lazarus came forth, bound hand and foot with the graveclothes, and Jesus said, "Loose him, and let him go!" We leave to your imagination the happy reunion that night in the home at Bethany.

Heaven, I think, will be just like that—just as simple and just as real—father there; mother there; brothers there; sisters there; and all the dear old memories about us.

SCENE III: A BANQUET

The last scene in which the two sisters appear is the banquet which was served for Christ at Bethany, no doubt a feast of commemoration and thanksgiving for the resurrection of Lazarus. This is the same banquet of which Matthew tells us, only he says it was in the house of Simon the Leper, and does not give the name of the woman who poured out the ointment. But it is clear that it is the same supper John speaks of when he says, "They made him a supper; and Martha served." The same capable Martha, taking full charge of the important banquet. All the disciples were there; Martha was there; Lazarus was there; and, best of all, Jesus was there. How wonderful to them to sit by the side of a man who had been among the dead, and by the side of Him who brought him back. What were the thoughts of Lazarus?

When Lazarus left his charnel-cave,
    And home to Mary's house return'd,
    Was this demanded—if he yearn'd
To hear her weeping by his grave?

"Where wert thou, brother, those four days?"
    There lives no record of reply,
    Which telling what it is to die
Had surely added praise to praise.

From every house the neighbors met,
    The streets were fill'd with joyful sound,
    A solemn gladness even crown'd
The purple brows of Olivet.

Behold a man raised up by Christ!
    The rest remaineth unreveal'd;
    He told it not; or something seal'd
The lips of that Evangelist.[1]

And Mary was there, although not in evidence at first. But there is no doubt as to what her thoughts were.

[1] Tennyson, *In Memoriam.* xxxi.

Her eyes are homes of silent prayer,
　　Nor other thought her mind admits
　　But, he was dead, and there he sits,
And he that brought him back is there.

Then one deep love doth supersede
　　All other, when her ardent gaze
　　Roves from the living brother's face,
And rests upon the Life indeed.[2]

It was a notable banquet, I am sure. Martha
would see to that. The best the market of Jerusalem could supply was there. But that was not enough
for Mary. Something more was due her Lord than
baked meats and costly drinks. She had purchased
a pound of ointment, very costly, the most expensive
she could buy. Waiting her opportunity, she broke
the vessel and poured the dark, luxurious ointment
over the feet of Jesus as he reclined at the table.
Then with the tresses of her hair she wiped his feet.
"And the house was filled with the odor of the ointment"—and the world has been filled with it ever
since.

Some of the disciples, led by Judas, complained
about this waste. But Jesus answered their indignation by telling them that Mary had anointed him
against the day of his death and burial. Then came
that great sentence, which endowed Mary's deed

[2] *Ibid.,* xxxii.

[83]

with fadeless immortality: "Verily I say unto **you**, Wheresoever this gospel shall be preached throughout the whole world, this also that she hath done shall be spoken of for a memorial of her."

Men did other acts of kindness for Christ. One lent him his boat, another his house, another his beast, another his strength, another his cup, and another his grave. Men were to witness for him and suffer for him and die for him; but the only deed done to Christ upon which he pronounced an immortality of fame was what Mary of Bethany did that night at the supper when she poured the ointment on his feet and dried them with her hair. Yes, Mary chose the better part, the good part. She chose to give her heart to Christ, and therefore she lives forever.

Woman, you are a sister to Mary; that is what Christ asks of you. He desires your love. He asks for your heart. Has no man ever asked for your hand? But here is the One altogether lovely, the chiefest among ten thousand. He comes and asks for your heart. Will you give it to him?

THE ONE THING NEEDFUL

Mary chose that good part, that one thing needful which could not be taken from her. Have you the one thing needful? Have you chosen that good part, which is salvation through faith in Christ? That is the one thing and the only thing, that is needful. Other things may be helpful, convenient, desirable, useful; but only one thing is needful, one thing without which you cannot do; that is saving faith in the Lord Jesus Christ. Sometimes you read the obituaries of men in the newspapers, telling of what they have done in life, institutions they have founded, books they have written, factories they have built, money they have had to leave behind them; but what about the one thing needful? Did they have that?

Saving faith in Christ is the "good part," which cannot be taken from you. All other things will be taken from you—health, money, beauty, fame, pleasure, and friends. Time and death will remove all these things, but not that better part. Have you chosen it, definitely, finally, irrevocably, and gladly —that better part? If not, will you choose it today? If you do, I can see Martha and Mary and Lazarus standing before the Throne, and I can hear them mention your name as they say to their Lord, "Lord, another soul has chosen that good part."

VI

THE WOMAN WHO SHEARED HIM

"And she made him sleep upon her knees."
JUDGES 16:19

A DANGEROUS PLACE TO SLEEP, FOR OUT OF THAT sleep none ever wakes but to weep. Out of that slumber men awake to find it is not morning, but midnight. And how dark that night!

Samson is the great humorist of the Bible. He was the perpetrator of huge practical jokes, as when he carried off the gates of Gaza and stacked them up on top of the hill near Hebron. In the horse-and-buggy days, when people still had gates about their homes, that was always the chief Hallowe'en prank, to carry off the gates and set them up on top of a high building. All this, I suppose, was an echo of Samson's ancient joke.

Another bit of horseplay of Samson was to choose for his weapon the jawbone of an ass, and with that weapon smite the Philistines, hip and thigh, with a great slaughter. But perhaps the most famous of his exploits and practical jokes was to catch three hundred foxes, tie them tail to tail, and, setting a firebrand between the tails, turn them loose in the barley fields of the Philistines. Joker, riddle propounder, doer of great exploits—it was not until the very last hour of his life that Samson began to take life seriously, and then it was almost too late. Like Samson, a great many people never wake up to the earnestness and seriousness of life until life is almost over.

But Samson is more than the great joker of the Bible. He is one of its supreme tragedies, one of its saddest shipwrecks, one of its outstanding exhibitions of the deep, deep pathos of life—of powers prostituted, talent debased, and genius soiled. The secret of that shipwreck was a woman—to be correct, several women, but one in particular—that Delilah upon whose knees Samson slept when his head was sheared of its golden locks and his divinely bestowed strength departed from him. Delilah is one of several temptresses who appear in the Bible. The other notorious ones are Potiphar's wife, who tempted Joseph; Jezebel, who stirred up Ahab; and Herodias, who tempted Herod. No series of sermons on the great women of the Bible would be complete without a sermon on Delilah; for, if the other women in this series illustrate woman's higher nature, her beautiful and beneficent influence over men, her power to stir the ambitions, to incite to deeds of heroism and valor and power, to launch a thousand ships, Delilah illustrates another power in woman just as real, her influence over man for the power of evil, turning him back from his high undertaking, obscuring the dawn of his ambition, putting out the stars of his hope, and stripping him of his strength and his honor. That frequently happens in life. The Bible is a book that holds the mirror up to life. Therefore, in the Bible we find the story of this beautiful temptress, Delilah.

Every life represents a purpose of God. Sin, alas, thwarts and mars and destroys that divine purpose in many a life. Nevertheless, it is important, and it is inspiring, to remember that you and your life represent a plan and purpose of God. Are you living up to that purpose? That was the way Samson came into the world. He was born for a purpose; and that purpose was to deliver Israel out of the hand of its oppressors, the cruel and blasphemous Philistines. Yet even in the angel's announcement of Samson's birth there was a prediction of the sorrow and tragedy of his life, for the angel said to Samson's mother, "He shall *begin* to deliver Israel." That was all that Samson did. He only began to save Israel. The morning of his life was bright; but soon that brightness was overclouded with gloom.

They called him Samson, "Sunshine," when he was born into that home in Israel. That is a good name for every child. How God, from hour to hour, from day to day, from week to week and month to month, from year to year and age to age, alleviates the sorrow and gloom of the world and penetrates its darkness with sunshine by the birth of little children!

Manoah and his wife asked the angel how they should bring this child up: "How shall we order the child, and how shall we do unto him?" The angel answered that the child was to be a Nazarite from his mother's womb, which meant that he was to drink no wine nor strong drink, and that no razor was to come upon his head. It is worth noting that the strongest man of the Old Testament, Samson, and the greatest man, according to Jesus, of the New Testament, John the Baptist, were both total abstainers. There was a law in Israel that no tool or instrument of iron was to be lifted over an altar, for the altar was dedicated to God. The Nazarite was a dedicated, consecrated man, and for that reason no shears or metal razor was to be lifted over his head. His unshorn locks were not the source of his strength, but the sign of his devotion to the will of God. That is an uplifting and sublime view of man's life. Man is an altar man. He ought to live for God. Keep that in mind! You are an altar man, an altar woman. Revere thyself! If you want the respect and reverence of others, revere and respect your own life. Have for yourself what John Milton tells us in his college days was a wall of defense about him against the vice and temptations of the college—"a just and pious reverence for my own person."

Now arrived at full manhood, Samson began to do exploits. After he made his first successful assault upon the oppressors of his country, his own people, stricken with an inferiority complex, and in dread of the Philistines, came to him and said, "Knowest thou not that the Philistines are rulers over us? what is this that thou hast done unto us?" Much that Samson did was wicked and sinful, according to our standards today; but give him credit for this—he had a hero in his soul. When all his countrymen cowered before the Philistines, he smote out at them in the name of God.

But a thing happened that happens to most young men. Samson fell in love. This was the first of three love affairs in Samson's life, the first of the three women who betrayed him and did him injury. Samson was a giant in strength and a hero in courage; but, as we shall presently see, he had his weak side. He was not able to say "No" to a woman. History abounds with men who, in certain respects, tower like giants above their fellow men—men like Lord Nelson, the hero of Trafalgar, and like Napoleon, who nevertheless were themselves easily conquered on one side of their life.

WOMAN NO. I

This woman down in Timnath was a Philistine. You can imagine the consternation when Samson, returning from there, announced to his father and mother that he had fallen in love with a Philistine maiden and that he intended to marry her! All their entreaties and prayers and protests and warnings against such an ill-advised alliance with a woman who belonged to the deadly enemies of Samson's country fell, as they often do, upon deaf ears. Samson wanted her. "I like her," he says; "I'll look after the future. Don't worry about that. Get her for me to wife."

One would have thought that Samson was big enough and strong enough to get a wife for himself, but that was the way they did things in those days. His parents agreed to arrange the betrothal, and Samson in high feather went down to visit his beloved. On the way down a lion roared against him, but in the exultation of his spirits at that time a lion was nothing to Samson, and seizing the lion he tore him asunder as one would a piece of paper. When he made his next visit to Timnath, bees had swarmed in the carcass of the lion; and, dipping in his rod, Samson tasted of the honey. That suggested to him a joke and riddle for the feast which he gave to the Philistine young men before his marriage, like the dinner a man about to be married gives to his male friends. When they asked him to entertain them with some story or joke, Samson said, "All right, I will lay a wager with you. If you can guess my riddle within seven days, I will give you thirty changes of garments. If you cannot, then you give the thirty changes of garments to me." They said: "All right, Samson. Put forth thy riddle. Let us hear it." And this was the riddle, which shows that Samson's strength was not all in his body and that he was well endowed above his shoulders: "Out of the eater came forth meat, and out of the strong came forth sweetness." Day after day the young Philistine blades debated and worked in vain over that riddle. Then they went to Samson's bride and ordered her, upon threat of death, to entice Samson and get from him the secret of his riddle.

Now we see where Samson was weak. He did not yield at first; but after his bride came at him for seven days, weeping all through those seven days, and telling him that if he loved her he would tell her, Samson yielded and told her the riddle. When the seven days were up the young Philistines appeared before Samson with a look of confidence and said to him: "We know your riddle, Samson. What is sweeter than honey, and what is stronger than a lion?" Samson kept his promise and gave the thirty changes of garments to the young Philistines; but he turned it into one of his famous jokes by getting the garments from the backs of Philistines whom he had slain. The upshot of that first romance of Samson was that his wife was given to his companion "whom he had used as his friend." Samson was betrayed by his friend and mocked and betrayed by his wife.

WOMAN NO. II

"We live and learn," the old saying has it. But some men never learn. Samson's next woman friend was a much worse woman, as far as her station was concerned, than the first one. This time it was a harlot in Gaza. The Philistines were told of a visit he made at the home of this woman, and that night they surrounded the house and said, "When it is day, we shall kill him." They were both right and wrong in their prediction. Samson escaped that time, and celebrated his escape by carrying off the gates of Gaza in mockery and setting them up on top of a high hill near the city. Nevertheless, Samson, although unknown to himself, had weakened his character. These indulgences in sin were "softening" him for the final kill. It has been said that hell is paved with good intentions. It is well to remember, however, that there is always a path that leads to hell before one gets there, and that path is paved with bad intentions and with bad deeds and bad associations. Yes, Philistines, plotting for the death of

Samson, you were right when you said, "When it is day, we shall kill him." You did not kill him, however; but sensuality did. When the night of indulgence and passion and sin is gone, then comes the dawn of judgment and retribution. "When it is day, we shall kill him!"

WOMAN NO. III

Samson's narrow escape from the Philistines at Gaza had taught him no wisdom. Now comes the third woman—the one who accomplishes the final overthrow of Samson. "And it came to pass afterward, that he loved a woman in the valley of Sorek, whose name was Delilah." This woman was undoubtedly the most beautiful and beguiling of all three. The Philistines rejoiced when they heard that Samson was waiting upon Delilah. "Now," they said, "we will get him. This time he shall not escape." So they went to her house and offered her a bribe of eleven hundred pieces of silver—$25,000 —if she would get out of Samson the secret of his great strength. It was the money that did the business with Delilah. Perhaps when she gave her consent she said to herself, "I can feel that when I do this it is a patriotic deed, for I am delivering into the hands of the Philistines the great enemy of my country." But it was the money that did the business. She thought of the chariots and horses she could have, the fine villa down by the seashore, the Ethiopian slaves to wait on her, the rich garments dyed with Tyrian dye, the gold of Ophir and the jewels of India.

Then Delilah went to work on Samson. There is no reason to think that these four teasings of Samson, these assaults upon his honor, took place in immediate succession, or on the same day and at the same visit. Very likely there were four successive visits that Samson paid to Delilah, and each time she beset him with her blandishments, her intoxicating beauty, and her guile. The first time, when Samson was in good humor, she said to him, "Samson, I have often admired this wonderful strength of yours. How the fame of it has gone through all this part of the world! There is not a man among the Philistines who could in the least way match you. I would like to know, Samson, the secret of this great strength, and I am sure you will tell me; for, of course, you can count on my confidence. I will never mention it to anyone else."

You can see the look in Delilah's eyes and hear the soft tone of her seducing voice as she says this to Samson. It is clear that Samson has no thought whatever of disclosing to Delilah, much as he loves her, the secret of his strength. What it suggests to him is the perpetration of another joke on the Philistines. So he tells Delilah that if she will bind him with seven green withes that have never been dried, he will be weak just as another man. Delilah passed this out to the Philistines; and the next time Samson came to pay her a visit she produced the green withes and, reminding Samson of what he had told her, bound him tightly with them—one of her slaves, no doubt, assisting her the while. You can see Samson smile to himself as the seven green withes are tightly fastened about his arms and his legs. Then, after a while, coming in suddenly upon Samson—superb actress that she was—with a tone of feigned alarm and concern for her huge lover, Delilah shouts, "Samson, the Philistines be upon thee!" With that Samson sprang to his feet, breaking his bonds as a thread of tow is broken when it is touched with fire. The Philistines, dreading the power of the aroused giant, fled before him.

The next time Samson came down, Delilah again set to work on him. She reproached him for mocking her and telling her lies, but in a tone of voice that must have pleased and flattered Samson. Still he has no thought of revealing to her the secret of his strength, and only thinks of another good joke he can play upon the Philistines. This time he tells her to bind him with new ropes that have never been used. At a subsequent visit, new ropes were in readiness, and Delilah and her slaves proceeded to bind Samson with those ropes. Again she came hurriedly in on him shouting, "The Philistines be upon thee!" and again Samson leaped to his feet, breaking the new ropes like threads, and rushed out against the fast-retreating Philistines.

Unwarned, and still confident, not only in his strength, but in his ability to keep the secret of it to himself, Samson makes yet another visit to the siren of the valley of Sorek. Delilah again reproaches him with her soft voice for mocking her and deceiving her, and again begs him to tell the secret of his strength. This time Samson tells her to weave the seven locks of his hair with the web and fasten it with the pin, and then he will be weak like other men. He was coming a little nearer—indeed, dangerously near—to the truth; for the secret of his strength— rather, the sign and symbol of it—was in his hair. Delilah rolled out the spinning wheel with the loom and the beam and, as the shuttle played to and fro, took the seven braids of Samson's hair and wove them to the beam, and then clamped it down with the pin. Excusing herself for a little while, she returned and in feigned excitement cried out, "Samson, the Philistines be upon thee!" Again Samson, awakened out of his sleep—for he had so enjoyed having his hair woven in to the beam by the soft hands of Delilah that he had gone to sleep—rose up in his might, carrying web, beam, loom, wheel, and all with him, and with the whole contraption clattering about his gigantic shoulders, rushed out upon the liers in wait.

Three victories over the Philistines and his three-fold resistance to the wiles of Delilah probably made Samson feel that he was invincible. If there was any voice of conscience that warned him, he probably said to himself, "I'll take the chance. I came pretty near to telling Delilah the last time; but this time I'll deceive her altogether. I'll go down to see her just once more." But, as is frequently the case, "just once more" was too often, for when Samson came this last time she assumed wounded feelings, and, with easily produced tears, said to Samson, "You don't really love me. If you did, you would hide nothing from me, but tell me all that is in your heart, and let me know the secret of your strength." This time, moved by her appeal to his affection, Samson spoke the fatal word, yet never expecting that his strength would go from him. He had been strong for so many years that he never thought that even his shorn locks would deprive him of his strength. Then he "told her all his heart." If his hair were cut he would be weak as other men. He must have had some little self-reproach, I think, as he spoke of his youth and of his mother. The thought of one's mother has often saved a man on the very edge of the pit and the abyss. But not here. Samson told Delilah—and when he did so he must have thought of the difference between this painted beauty and his godly mother—that he had been a Nazarite unto God from his mother's womb.

Delilah felt sure that this time she had the secret of his strength, and sent word to the Philistines to post themselves near her chamber and be ready for action. Then she put him to sleep upon her knees. His great golden locks hung down to the floor. That fatal sleep! Samson, look up at the blue Syrian sky, visible through the window of Delilah's chamber, for you will never see it again! Samson, look upon the golden sun in the heavens, for you will never look upon the sun again! Samson, look upon those brawny arms of thine—those arms which have done such great exploits for God—for you will never see them again! Samson, look upon the beautiful, bewitching countenance of that Delilah who bends over thee, for never again will you look upon her face! Out of this sleep, Samson, you will awaken to blindness and degradation.

And that was what happened. While he slept, Delilah's slave sheared off his golden hair. The Philistines came rushing in as Delilah shouted to him, "The Philistines be upon thee!" Samson stirred himself, for "he wist not that the Lord was departed from him," and thought he could easily conquer his enemies as he had done so many times before. But the moment he stood on his feet he realized that something had gone from him. He was weak just

like any other *ordinary* man! The Philistines overcame him, bored out his eyes, and carried him off to
the dungeon, where they set him to the work of the
ass, grinding in the mill.

HOW MEN FALL

"Samson wist not that the Lord was departed from
him." Something infinitely sad about that! Perhaps you have heard a great musician who played
after his skill was gone, or a great singer who sang
after her voice was gone. Some years ago I heard a
preacher who in his prime was able to stir thousands;
but now the fire had sunk, his power had departed
from him. There was not the least tone in his voice,
or flame in his countenance, or flash in his eye, to sug-
gest the great preacher of not so many years before.
Time had taken, as it always must, its deadly toll.
There is a pathos about departed strength, in that
sense; but oh, how much deeper is the pathos of departed moral and spiritual strength!

Samson did not lose his strength all in one day, or
in one rash promise to the Philistine courtesan. No;
it had been steadily ebbing from him. That is the
way men lose their moral and spiritual strength. A
great tree stands yonder in the fields. Its leaves are
green; its trunk appears to be sound and strong.
Then suddenly, when the great wind blows, the tree
goes down with a crash and leaves a lonely place

against the sky. But when the tree is fallen you can see that it was rotten within. It was just waiting for the sufficiently strong wind to bring it down in ruins. So men sink slowly and gradually to their ruin. When the crisis of a strong temptation comes upon them, and the cry goes up, "The Philistines be upon thee!" then they go down.

ENEMIES ALWAYS WAITING

The moment Samson revealed the true secret of his strength to Delilah, the liers in wait were ready for him. There are always "liers in wait"—enemies of your soul—waiting for you, ready to rush in when you lower the shield of your defense as Samson did. And what was that shield of Samson's defense? It was his consecration to God, of which his hair was only the sign and token. Whoever lets the thought of God pass out of his mind has, as it were, parted with his hair, the secret of his strength; and the enemies of the soul will quickly overcome him. Therefore, my soul, be on thy guard. Live as if in the presence of God. Test daily your consecration to him. Samson went down when he let go of God. But Joseph, greatly tempted by another wicked woman, won his victory and lives forever an example to young men and young women because he would not let go from him the thought of God and his obligations to God. In the dreadful moment of his temptation he cried out, "How then can I do this great wickedness and sin against God?"

Let anyone whose locks are now being toyed with remember Samson and be warned by what happened to him. A moment's consent, and then the degradation, the slavery, and the long darkness.

A BRIGHT SUNSET

Sometimes you have seen an autumn or winter day that rose in beauty and splendor and then, ere midday had come, was clouded and darkened. But in the late afternoon, just before night came, the sun appeared and there was a bar of flaming gold across the western horizon. That is what I think of when I read the life of Samson. Just before his death, the sun comes out again. The Philistines had assembled in the temple of their god Dagon to celebrate their victory over Israel and their conquest of Israel's great champion, the blind Samson. Suddenly a roar goes up from the half-drunken lords and ladies: "Bring in Samson! Let him make sport for us!" Samson is brought out of his dungeon, a boy leading him by the hand. He is a huge figure of a man with his hair grown again and hanging over his shoulders, but with sad, sightless eyes. At the command of his keepers he makes sport for the Philistines. Among those Philistines who lean over the parapet of the gallery I see a face that poor, blind

Samson cannot see. It is the face of Delilah!—the cruel, coldly beautiful, licentious face of Delilah. And in that face not a look of pity or compassion! Listen, as she shouts down some taunt or mockery at her erstwhile lover.

JUST THIS ONCE!

But wait! Samson's hair has grown again. But something more important than that has taken place. Samson has repented. Samson has come back to God. He asks the boy who conducts him to let him feel and lean against the two main pillars that uphold the balustrade and the gallery. As he stands there he puts one great arm about this marble pillar and another great arm about the other marble pillar; and then, in a voice which was lost in the hubbub of the drinking and jeering Philistines, but not lost to God, Samson makes his last and beautiful and pathetic prayer: "O Lord God, remember me, I pray thee, and strengthen me, I pray thee, only this once, O God!" With that his arms tighten around those pillars. One mighty heave and pull, and the pillars are pulled from their sockets, and down in one red roar of ruin crashes the temple of Dagon, burying in death the blasphemous Philistines—and Samson, too, for he had gladly asked to die that he might strike one last blow for God. And there by the side of the dead Samson I see another face, and another form, all covered with blood, and blackened with the dust of ruin. Whose is it? It is the face of the temptress Delilah. Now, Delilah, you have had your wish! You have learned what the secret of Samson's strength is, and how dreadful that strength can be in judgment and retribution. It is the strength of repentance and faith in God.

"O Lord, God, remember me, I pray thee, and strengthen me, I pray thee, only this once." That may be your need, your desperate need. You have forgotten God. You have broken his commandments. You have sinned against him. But God is merciful. He will in no wise cast out that man that cometh unto him. Call on him now. Pray as Samson did, "O Lord God, remember me, I pray thee, and strengthen me, I pray thee, only this once." Yes, thanks be unto God, "only this once." Only one heartfelt prayer for forgiveness, only one courageous and sincere choice and decision for the right, and that "only once" can be stretched into never-ending eternity of happiness and joy.

VII

THE WOMAN WHO MARRIED THE WRONG MAN

"She was a woman of good understanding, and of a beautiful countenance: but the man was churlish and evil in his doings."
I Samuel 25:3

"It was a mistake," she said as I greeted her, a friend of former years, as she came out of the pew. She had been married since I saw her last, and naturally I made some allusion to her marriage. But that was her only comment, as a look of sadness came into her face—"It was a mistake." Like many another woman, she had married the wrong man. And she was not the first, nor the last, to do that. There are all kinds of husbands and wives, and all kinds of marriages; and the Bible would not have been the complete book that it is, and the perfect mirror of life that it is, had it not had a story of a woman who married the wrong man.

There are, indeed, plenty of men who married the wrong woman. Job is a classic example of that; for when things were at their worst for Job, his wife, instead of encouraging him and strengthening him, told him to curse God and die. One of the wisest of men, Socrates, married a scold. Charles Dickens, the man who touches all the chords of the heart in its relationship to the home, married the wrong woman. John Wesley was one of the saintliest of men, but he married the wrong woman, if ever man did. But more numerous and more tragic are the number of women who married the wrong man.

Here in this masterpiece of Old Testament biography we have the story of the Beauty and the Beast. Sometimes you have seen a charming, gracious lady married to a boorish, churlish, cruel, wicked man; and you have wondered how it ever could have happened. But in ancient days you would not have wondered so much, for the woman had comparatively little to say as to whom she would marry. That was arranged for her. Particularly would she have little to say about the matter when the husband was a rich man like Nabal; for "the man was very great, and he had three thousand sheep, and a thousand goats." Then one did not say a man was worth so many thousand dollars or pounds, but so many sheep, oxen, camels, goats.

It was a sad marriage for Abigail, as such marriages often are. In a town in California where I spent a year as a boy, I used to see riding down the avenue every morning near our house a large man mounted on a magnificent sorrel horse, with a great mastiff following after him. But the man's reputation was not good. He had married the daughter of a minister, and one wondered how she could be happy. In the old pagan days men used to deck the oxen devoted for sacrifice with garlands and ribbons. But that did not keep back the gleaming knife of the priest when he slew them at the altar. Neither does wealth, station, or a great name hold back the knife of unhappiness when a woman is married to a man like Nabal.

It was sheepshearing time in Carmel, a still, green and pleasant country south of Hebron. And what a shearing time it was—three thousand of Nabal's sheep to be shorn of their fleecy wool. Everywhere the ground about Carmel was white, not with snow, but with the wool of the shorn sheep; and everywhere one could hear the bleating of the sheep and the sound of the clippers. From all parts of the nearby country the people had gathered to assist in the ritual of the sheepshearing; and just as in the early days on the American farms the barnraising or the threshing season was a time of social intercourse, of joy as well as labor, when the tables groaned with plenty, and there was singing, and sometimes dancing, so in ancient Palestine—and still today—the sheepshearing season was a time of festive joy and reunion, of feasting and drinking and the giving of gifts.

The news spread through the land that Nabal was shearing his three thousand sheep. At that time

David, pursued by the relentless and sleepless jealousy of Saul, in whose place he had been anointed king, had taken refuge in the south country, gathering about him a band of several hundred young men who were willing to share the hardship and excitement of David's life. The kingship must then have seemed far off to David—so much so that Jonathan had to go to David secretly at night in the wood of Ziph and strengthen his hand in God and restore his faith that God would make him king over Israel.

Some of David's followers brought word to him that Nabal was shearing his sheep. That reminded David that no matter what hill they had climbed or what valley they had penetrated Nabal was the man whose flocks they had encountered. They had never molested his flocks, but had protected them against raiding and thieving Bedouins. It was the fine custom of the ancient shearing season that the man whose sheep were being sheared should give gifts to all as a token of thanks to God and of good will to his neighbors. With this in mind, David dispatched some of his young men to greet Nabal and to receive from him the usual present.

The sheepsharing and the accompanying festivities were well under way when David's messengers arrived. All about the sheepshearing platforms are pitched the black tents of the people who have come with their families and their animals—camels, sheep, goats. The red, yellow, and blue headdresses of the women are brilliant in the Syrian sunlight. In groups of six, ten, twenty, the sheep are driven first into the pools to be washed. Thence they are driven up to the shearing place, where they are thrown down on the platforms while the shearers, holding them between their knees, clip from them their thick and infinitely soft garments that man may be clothed and warmed.

After watching for a time, and perhaps lending a hand themselves, the messengers of David make their way to where Nabal sits drinking under his pavilion. They state their errand on behalf of David, and also notify Nabal how David has protected his flocks. But when Nabal hears their request, the churlish fool breaks out into an angry insult: "Who is David, and who is the son of Jesse? There be many servants that break away nowadays from their masters. For all I know, David, this son of Jesse, may be one of those fugitive slaves, skulking about the country, stealing and poaching. Do you think I am going to take my bread and my water and my flesh that I have killed for my shearers and give it to a set of vagabonds?"

The coarse insult was all the more offensive because of the Oriental laws of courtesy, which require politeness, under certain circumstances, even to a man's deadly enemy. When the young men brought word back to David how Nabal had received them and what he had said to them, David was beside himself with rage. His ruddy countenance blanched as the wave of anger swept over him. Drawing his sword, and turning to his six hundred men, David gave his angry command, "Gird ye on every man his sword!" David was by nature a kind, generous, loving, magnanimous man; but, like all strong characters, he was capable of great indignation, and when once roused, his anger and rage could carry him to terrible lengths.

It looked as if it was going to be so on this occasion. Marching at the head of his men, David started for Carmel, fierce revenge flaming in his heart. As he marched along, and heard behind him the tread of his armed men, their swords clanking on their thighs, he said to himself, or probably spoke aloud so that his men might hear: "Never heard of David, never heard of the son of Jesse, did he? Thinks we are runaway slaves, vagabonds, eh? Well, we will teach him a lesson. Before the night comes down, Nabal and all his people will find out who David is. God do so to me and more also, if Nabal or any of his household is left alive by morning!" Thus he planned not only revenge on the churlish Nabal, but the destruction of all his people. And with great satisfaction David listened to the tramp, tramp, tramp of his soldiers behind him.

But there was another procession on the march that day. Frightened servants of Nabal had brought word to their mistress, Abigail, of their master's coarse insult to David. Abigail knew what was coming. David was not the man to let such an affront go unpunished. She might have taken steps to protect only herself; but in the nobility and kindness of her nature she made haste to save from death and vengeance the innocent household of Nabal, and even that wicked man himself. Did a voice say to her, "Now, Abigail, is your chance! Now is your chance to be rid of that drunken fool and beast to whom you have been joined all these years. Do not stand in the way of David's vengeance, and all will be well with you"? If such a voice spoke, if such a desire rose up for a moment, the high-minded Abigail quickly suppressed it and turned all her wits and energies and charms to save Nabal and his household from death—and also, as we shall see, to save David from himself.

Summoning her servants, she bade them load the animals with presents for David's men—cheese, wine, bread, raisins—and, mounted on her own beast, she led the caravan in the direction from which David was marching. So the two caravans, the two processions—one the procession of anger and revenge, the other the procession of peace and forgiveness and reconciliation—approached each other.

At the covert of one of the hills, just as the morning mists were lifting, the two processions met. Dismounting from her animal, and hurrying to where David stood with angry threatening mien, his hand on his sword, Abigail bowed before him and commenced her beautiful and immortal plea.

If you leave out the speeches of our Lord, there are two which are the most famous and eloquent speeches and addresses of the Bible. First of all, there is the wonderful speech that Judah made to Joseph in Egypt, when the still-disguised Joseph was threatening to keep Benjamin as a hostage, and Judah pled with him for the sake of their aged father to have mercy, saying that if Benjamin did not return it would bring the gray hairs of their father Jacob down in sorrow to the grave. That speech made Joseph, polished statesman of Egypt, break down in uncontrolled tears; and to read it even today brings a lump to the throat. The other most eloquent speech of the Bible is this beautiful plea that lovely Abigail made with David to keep back his hand from blood and vengeance. Perhaps in heaven it will be permitted me, when I meet Judah, to ask him to go apart for a little from the company of Jacob and his brethren and sit down with me, under one of the trees of life by the river of water of life, and repeat for me that wonderful speech he made to Joseph; and perhaps, if David can spare

her from his side for ten minutes, I can persuade
Abigail to go over again, with that lovely voice and
lovely face, the speech she made that morning to David by the covert of the hill.

Let me repeat now for you that whole speech, for
it is so eloquent that we must not lose a single word
of it:

Upon me, my lord, upon me let this iniquity be:
and let thine handmaid, I pray thee, speak in thine
audience, and hear the words of thine handmaid. Let
not my lord, I pray thee, regard this man of Belial,
even Nabal: for as his name is, so is he; Nabal is his
name, and folly is with him: but I thine handmaid saw
not the young men of my lord, whom thou didst send.
Now therefore, my lord, as the Lord liveth, and as
thy soul liveth, seeing the Lord hath withholden thee
from coming to shed blood and from avenging thyself with thine own hand, now let thine enemies, and
they that seek evil to my lord, be as Nabal. And now
this blessing which thine handmaid hath brought unto
my lord, let it even be given unto the young men that
follow my lord. I pray thee, forgive the trespass of
thine handmaid: for the Lord will certainly make my
lord a sure house; because my lord fighteth the battles
of the Lord, and evil hath not been found in thee all
thy days. Yet a man is risen to pursue thee, and to
seek thy soul: but the soul of my lord shall be bound
in the bundle of life with the Lord thy God; and the
souls of thine enemies, them shall he sling out, as out
of the middle of a sling. And it shall come to pass,
when the Lord shall have done to my lord according to

all the good that he hath spoken concerning thee, and shall have appointed thee ruler over Israel; that this shall be no grief unto thee, nor offence of heart unto my lord, either that thou hast shed blood causeless, or that my lord hath avenged himself; but when the Lord shall have dealt well with my lord, then remember thine handmaid.

It was not strange that David melted before that speech. Not only did he turn back from his errand of blood and revenge, but he blessed God for the providence that had sent Abigail to meet him. Thrusting his sword into its scabbard, David gave the order to his men to countermarch to their own encampment—which they were willing enough to do, having listened with rapt countenance to the moving words of Nabal's wife.

Nabal had been spared; his household had been spared; and David himself had been saved. When Abigail got home Nabal lay in a drunken stupor. The next day, when he was aroused out of his stupor, she told him what had happened. It is hard to tell whether it was out of anger at his beautiful wife's interference, or the shock of learning how narrowly he had escaped the vengeance of David; but when he heard the news, Nabal had a seizure— a stroke. His heart, it is said, became as stone, and in a few days he was dead.

The story has a pleasant, and not at all surprising, sequel. When David heard that Nabal was dead, he paid his court to the beautiful widow and soon thereafter married her; and never did a man make a happier choice. We know something of some of the other wives of David—Michal, who mocked at him, and Bathsheba, whom he loved well, but not wisely. We are glad that early in his history he had the counsel and affection and companionship of a woman like Abigail. Sometimes I think that Abigail cannot have lived long; for if she had, I feel sure she would have kept David from many of the deeds of folly and sin and cruelty which stained his reign, even as she did there by the covert of the hill when she kept him back from blood and death.

A WOMAN UNSOURED AND UNEMBITTERED BY ADVERSITY

When we come to sum up the truths which come home to us from the story of lovely Abigail, the first one that strikes us is this: she did not permit the trial and adversity of life to embitter her spirit. For such a woman to be married to such a beast must have been the sorest of trials. What could be greater? How poignant must have been the sorrow of Abigail when she awoke not many days after her marriage with the conviction that she had made a supreme mistake and had married a besotted fool and churl! But it is evident that she bore her cross with resignation. She did not become bitter or turn

[115]

GREAT WOMEN OF THE BIBLE

against life. The harder her experience, the sweeter her disposition. As certain trees when struck by the ax will answer only by sending forth sweet-smelling sap, so the keen edge of adversity and trial evoked from the soul of Abigail only peace and beauty. Her affliction, no doubt, seemed grievous to her; but afterward, as the apostle puts it, it yielded the peaceful fruits of righteousness. In your disappointment, your sore trial, your bitter grief, think of this woman and follow in her steps.

GOD'S PROVIDENCE IN OUR LIVES

Another truth that comes home to us from this brief but superb biography of Abigail is the providence of God in our daily life. I like that famous speech of Abigail, not only for its surpassing pathos and eloquence, but also because it stirs tender memories in my heart. That was the phrase oft upon my father's lips when he made the prayer in the old home at family worship, asking God that all his children might be bound up in the bundle of life. Earnest, simple, beautiful prayer, thou didst make for us, father. Long since, now, thy days have been rounded in a sleep. But not till they themselves sleep the last sleep will thy children forget thy accents as on bended knee thou didst intercede for us with God and ask that we with thee might be bound up forever in the bundle of life, safe at last in that everlasting home, where they go no more out and come no more in!

In her intercession with David, Abigail reassured him that God's hand was not withdrawn from him, and that, however dark and forbidding the present day, he would be king over Israel. What better can one do for another than that? to remind him that God has a purpose and a plan in his life, and that if he will but obey and trust in God, all things will finally work together for good. Perhaps you are discouraged, or even rebellious. God's way with you seems hard. Your life seems to you useless and all your efforts futile. Be of good cheer! God who created you has high things in store for you. Be faithful! Hold back your hand from evil and your heart from unbelief! Wait, I say, on the Lord, and be of good courage, and he will bring it to pass!

THE REGRETS WE HAVE MISSED, AND THOSE WE CAN MISS

The final truth we hear from the lips of this most eloquent preacher, Abigail, as she pleads with David, is that no one ever regrets the evil he did not do. To David she said, "Now seeing the Lord hath withholden thee from coming to shed blood"—for, you see, she assumes that David is going to heed her plea—"when the Lord shall have appointed thee ruler over Israel, this will be no grief unto thee, that

[117]

thou hast shed blood causeless." How true that was! Poor David had many things to regret when later in his life he looked back over its checkered history, many acts of revenge and folly and shame; but there was one thing that he did not need to regret, and that was that in an hour of insult and anger he avenged himself against Nabal by slaying, not only the insulter, but his whole family and house. Through the gentle plea of Abigail, and through his wise yielding to that plea, David was spared that one regret and remorse. Bitter as his cup was, that drop of bitterness was never mixed in it.

Think, friend, of the regrets you have missed. When you look at the scroll of yesterday I know there will be much that you will wish had not been written there. But do not forget the things that are not there—the things you might have had occasion to regret, but which are not there, because God, in his grace and providence, kept you back from them. And when you think of those things that are not there, thank God for it.

But think, alas, my friend, of the regrets that you might miss. Abigail told David of a regret he might miss if he would only listen to her advice. He listened and was spared that regret. Be wise, then, for your future. That noble woman said to David, "When you are king, it will be no regret to you that you kept back your hand from blood and vengeance." I appeal to you now on the ground of those things, that course of conduct, those choices and decisions, which you will never regret. It will be no regret to you that you did not forget God, but "remembered thy Creator in the days of thy youth," and in middle life, and in old age. It will be no regret to you that you did not neglect God's Word, God's Holy Day, God's House of Worship. It will be no regret to you that you did not forget the poor and the oppressed and the afflicted. It will be no regret to you that you did not yield to your angry passions. It will be no regret to you that you did not take a mean advantage for the sake of gain; but, rather, suffered loss. It will be no regret to you that, when insulted or persecuted or shamefully treated, you did not do as you had been done unto; but overlooked the wrong and forgave the wrongdoer. No! These things will never cause your soul regret. Answer me, enthroned and blessed saints in heaven, and tell me if any of these things caused you a moment's regret! I know what ye will say. I know that ye will answer that those deeds, those choices or decisions, those good things that you did, those evil things you did not, have rather brought you peace of spirit and added to your cup of joy in the heavenly places!

And one thing more I know you will never regret. You will never regret that, as David heeded the pleading of that beautiful woman, you heeded the pleading of God's Holy Spirit, and, repenting of all your sins, beholding Jesus Christ, the Son of God, wounded for your transgressions and bruised for your iniquities, gave your heart to him for time and for eternity—your Saviour, Guide, and Friend— and asked him to bind you up with him in the bundle of Eternal Life. Have you done that? Are you bound up in the bundle of Eternal Life? If you are not, then God's Holy Spirit pleads with you now and asks you to choose Eternal Life, not tomorrow, not next year, but now.

VIII

THE WOMAN WHO DECEIVED HER HUSBAND

> "And Rebekah took goodly raiment of her
> eldest son Esau, ... and put them upon
> Jacob her younger son."
>
> GENESIS 27:15

REBEKAH WAS THE WOMAN WHO DECEIVED HER husband. She was not the first to do that, nor the last. But that is not what one thinks of when one hears her name. More than any other woman in the Bible, Rebekah spelled romance; and her romance, beginning at the well in Mesopotamia, is all the more engaging because she was in love with a man she had never seen.

Sometimes people secure a reputation and fame not altogether in keeping with their real history and conduct. That is certainly so, to a degree, in the case of Rebekah; for the marriage service, in its concluding prayer, asks that "as Isaac and Rebekah lived faithfully together, so these persons may surely perform and keep the vow and covenant between them made." That was true, perhaps, in the early life of Isaac and Rebekah. But later on, as we shall see, there was a breach of faith on the part of Isaac and on the part of Rebekah.

The closing chapter of their relationship was anything but ideal. There the beautiful girl of Mesopotamia's well, who became Isaac's wife and comforted him after the death of his mother Sarah, has been transformed into a scheming old woman who cruelly deceives her blind and dying husband. And Isaac too has changed for the worse. He is no longer the winsome youth, the child of Abraham's and Sarah's old age, the central figure in the scene on Mount Moriah when Abraham was about to offer him up as a sacrifice; no longer the gentle dreaming youth who went out into the fields to meditate at the eventide, and was so engaged when the veiled Rebekah came with her camels; nor is he now the nonstriving, nonresisting Isaac, who when the herdsmen of Gerar stole the wells he had dug, did not strive with them, but removed elsewhere and called the place a name still borne by so many old-time country churches—"Rehoboth," there is room. Ah, if only the nations today would follow that policy of Isaac's, would realize that there is room for all; then the lips of the cannon would grow still, and the seas of blood would be dried up! No; it is not that winsome and attractive Isaac that we see in this closing scene, but a gluttonous old man, who wants a dish of venison before he dies.

Rebekah deceived her husband, for she was the chief architect in the whole miserable business. But that does not tell the whole story of Rebekah. There is no doubt that, despite her deception, Rebekah is one of the great women of the Bible—beautiful and romantic in her youth, strong and decided in her character, and even in the act of duplicity, where the curtain drops on her history, animated by a noble ambition and desire.

The story of Rebekah begins at an eastern well. Take out of the Bible the scenes at the well, and you have robbed it of much of its charm and beauty. It was at the well of Midian that the exiled Moses drove off the rude shepherds and drew water for the flocks of Zipporah, who turned out to be his future wife. It was at another Mesopotamian well that Jacob first kissed Rachel and waited fourteen years for another chance. It was near the well of Bethlehem that the fugutive David, his heart stirred with the tender memories of youth, sighed and said, "Oh that one would give me drink of the water of the well of Bethlehem, that is at the gate." And it was by the well of Jacob that Jesus sat down and talked with the woman of Samaria about the Water of Life.

Although it is always dangerous to try to retell the perfect tale, let us go back to that old well in Mesopotamia where the story of Rebekah had its beginning. The sun is sinking over the desert near the city of Nahor. Yonder, winding down from the southwest, comes a small caravan of camels. Seated on one of the camels is Eliezer, the chief servant of Abraham. Having had intimations that his end was not far off, Abraham had called his steward to him and made him swear that he would not permit Isaac to marry a woman of Canaan. He charged him to go down into the far east whence Abraham had come, and find a wife for Isaac among his own kindred and people. There was only one restraint laid upon the steward—he was not to let Isaac dwell in the eastern land, for God had promised to Abraham and his descendants the land of Canaan. Faithful to his vow and oath, Eliezer is on his way east to find Isaac a wife, for Isaac was a reticent, retiring young man who probably would never have been able to find one for himself. Here they come, swaying along the desert highway, the ten soft-footed camels of the chief steward laden with presents for the family of the as yet unknown bride to be. In obedience to the command of Eliezer the ten camels kneel down at the well outside the town of Nahor. It is at the eventide; and, according to the custom, the women come out from the gate of Nahor, their vessels on their heads, to draw water at the well.

When the steward saw them coming, he offered up a devout petition, asking God to grant him good fortune that day and give him a sign that he might know which of the young women he saw approaching the well was to be the bride of Isaac. What he asked was that the one to whom he should say, "Let down thy pitcher, I pray thee, that I may drink," and who should immediately respond, "Drink, and I will give thy camels drink also," would be the one God had appointed as Isaac's wife.

He had hardly concluded his prayer, when Rebekah, a niece of Abraham, and cousin to Isaac, came to the well with her pitcher upon her shoulder. She lowered her pitcher into the well and came up with it on her shoulder. As she did so, the servant of Abraham said to her, "Let me, I pray thee, drink a little water of thy pitcher." Rebekah at once answered, "Drink, my lord," and gave him to drink. Then she ran back to the well, and drawing water with her pitcher, poured it into the trough for the camels of the stranger.

WILT THOU GO?

Certain now that Rebekah was the chosen wife for Isaac, the steward presented her with a golden earring and golden bracelets, and inquired of her her name and family. When he learned that her family was related to that of Abraham, he was all the more satisfied in his mind, for Rebekah had good family background. She had grace and beauty, for it is said that she was "very fair to look upon";

she had courtesy, too, and hospitality, and vital vivacity, for everything she did, she did quickly. The old matchmaker bowed his head and gave thanks to God who had thus led and directed him to this beautiful girl.

When he made his proposal to Rebekah's brother, Laban—for the father seems to have been dead—Laban gave his consent, but said that Rebekah must make the final decision herself. When they had called Rebekah and explained to her why the man had come and what the proposal was, they said to her, "Wilt thou go with this man?" Without a moment's hesitation, Rebekah answered, "I will go!"

Down through the ages, over and over again, have echoed that question and that answer: "Wilt thou go?" "I will go!" Rebekah, Rachel, Sarah, Mary, ancient, medieval, and modern young woman, sought by the young man—all of you have answered that fundamental and momentous question, "Wilt thou go with this man?" Had you not, the world long ago would have ceased to move, and men would have ceased to praise God their Creator and Redeemer.

With the servant of Abraham and his caravan, Rebekah, trusting in God, traveled from Mesopotamia down to Canaan, where Isaac lived. She was deeply in love, as many young women have been, with a man she had never seen. It was not long after the death of Sarah, Isaac's loved mother; and

[126]

at the eventide Isaac was out in the fields meditating —grieving, no doubt, for his mother, as many a man after him has done, and wishing he could have her back, if only for an hour.

Riding on her camel, Rebekah saw Isaac in the distance and said to the servant, "What man is this that walketh in the field to meet us?" When she learned that it was Isaac, her future husband, she alighted from her camel and modestly covered her face with a veil. Thus Isaac first met his wife. The rest of the meeting the Bible tells best of all: "And Isaac brought her into his mother Sarah's tent, and took Rebekah, and she became his wife; and he loved her: and Isaac was comforted after his mother's death."

That was the beginning. Would that the rest of the story were as fair and charming as that first chapter. But I suppose that is rarely so in this world. Even this marriage, made in heaven, directed of God, had its less lustrous side. In the course of time two sons were born to Rebekah—Esau and Jacob. Isaac loved Esau, because he was a hunter and brought him game to eat from the field; but Rebekah—discerning, wise Rebekah—seeing the difference in the sons, and remembering how the Lord had said to her, "The elder shall serve the younger," loved Jacob.

By and by Esau married Judith, a Hittite woman.

To the ambitious, proud, and pious Rebekah that was a bitter blow, that her son should have married a heathen woman. It seemed to Rebekah that, by this union with the Hittite woman, Esau had renounced and repudiated all the promises which had come down through Abraham concerning a great future, and a great mission for God, and a great blessing for mankind; and she was determined that Jacob should not follow in his brother's steps. To Isaac, Rebekah said, "I am weary of my life because of the daughters of Heth: if Jacob take a wife of the daughters of Heth, ... what good shall my life do me?" Thus it is an old custom among proud, loving mothers to think sometimes that the woman their son has chosen for a wife is not worthy of him.

Rebekah noted that Isaac was getting weaker every day. At first he went just a little distance from the black tents on his daily walk. Then it was shortened and shortened, until he no longer stirred from the tent. One day she overheard him say to Esau that his end was not far off, and that he wanted him to take his bow and arrow and bring in a deer, so that he might eat the venison, and then bless him before he died. At once a cunning idea came into Rebekah's mind. The patriarchal blessing meant a great deal in those times. Isaac was blind and weak. Why not deceive him by substituting Jacob, and thus get the blessing for Jacob? Had not Esau proved himself unworthy of it, first by his marriage to a heathen woman, and then by selling the birthright to Jacob for a mess of pottage? And as for Isaac himself, probably Rebekah had ceased to respect him. How could she ever forget the despicable cowardice of Isaac when they were traveling through the land of the Philistines, and Isaac, fearful lest the Philistines, taken with the rare beauty of Rebekah, would kill him so that they might take her for a wife, passed Rebekah off as his sister? Recently a woman wrote to me, "I have married a man ten years older than myself whom I love and respect." It is always sad when those two do not go together—love and respect. Love sometimes lingers on, I suppose, even when respect is gone. But the ideal relationship is where the wife both loves and respects the husband and the husband loves and respects the wife.

With Rebekah, quick in old age as she had been at the well in her youth, to think was to act. Calling Jacob, she laid before him her plan. He was to kill two kids of the goats, and Rebekah would prepare them so that Isaac would not know the difference between the meat of the kid and venison. That would be easy. But Jacob was not sure about the rest. Jacob was a smooth man; Esau was hairy. What if blind Isaac should put out his hands to feel Jacob when he brought his father the meat and asked for the blessing! But Rebekah said she would see to that. Whatever blame or curse there might be for such a deception, she would bear it. "Upon me be thy curse, my son; only obey my voice." Then she put the skins of the kids upon his hands and upon the back of his neck; and thus disguised, Jacob went in to his father.

When Jacob saluted his father and gave him of the meat Rebekah had prepared, Isaac, whose ear was not as dull as his eye, thought that the voice sounded like that of Jacob. Wondering how Esau had shot and prepared a deer in so short a time, he said to Jacob, "Come near, I pray thee, that I may feel thee, my son, whether thou be my very son Esau or not." With his trembling hands Isaac felt of Jacob's arms, and then the back of his neck, but wherever his hand touched he felt the hairy skin of the kids. Perplexed, the old man said, "The voice is Jacob's voice, but the hands are the hands of Esau." Still unconvinced, he made one more pathetic appeal to Jacob: "Art thou my very son Esau?" And Jacob said, "I am." Then, having partaken of the meat, Isaac lifted his hands over the kneeling Jacob and bestowed upon him the blessing. "God give thee of the dew of heaven, and the fatness of the earth, and plenty of corn and wine: let people serve thee, and nations bow down to thee."

LIFE'S IRREVOCABLE

Thus Jacob cheated Esau of the blessing. And there, looking out from behind the fold of the tent, stands Rebekah, anxiously watching and listening to see if her plot succeeds, and if Jacob will get the blessing.

But the first scene was hardly over, and Rebekah had hardly spoken her whispered congratulations to Jacob, when Esau made his appearance, and coming to his father with the venison he had prepared, asked him to eat it and then bless him. The startled old man cried out, "Who art thou?" "I am Esau, thy first-born son," answered the surprised Esau. "Who?" cried the father. "If so, then who was it that brought me venison a little while ago, and upon whom I laid my hands in blessing?" Then they both knew what had happened. Jacob had stolen the blessing! Lifting up his voice with an exceeding bitter cry, Esau, realizing what it meant, said, "Bless me, even me also, O my father!" But Isaac could not now recall the blessing. Esau found no place for repentance, though he sought it carefully and with tears. The irrevocable had been done— yet, cheated and robbed and wronged though he was, Esau was but reaping the harvest of his own sin when he sold the birthright for a mess of pottage. Ah, those tears of Esau! Those tears of Esau!

Those bitter, bitter tears! Those tears of unavailing remorse and regret!

I hear that bitter cry of Esau echoed in David's cry, "I have sinned." I hear it echoed in the cry of Judas as he flings down the thirty pieces of silver at the feet of the high priest, saying, "I have sinned!" I hear it echoed in the remorse of the son who has neglected his parents, in the remorse of the husband who has wronged and outraged his wife. I hear the echo of that lament in the cry of the man who has sullied his soul in youth, and now cannot wash out the stains. I hear it echoed in the cry of that great number who, like Esau, put the appetite of the moment above the eternal satisfactions of the soul, and started a sequence of events which no power can ever stop. I hear the echo of that cry in the lament of one who has in a passion spoken fearful words which now can never be recalled.

Turn back, turn back, then, before you cry that bitter, bitter cry of Esau, and discover that there are some things which are irrevocable. Beware of the irrevocable on the wrong side of life. Choose rather the irrevocable on the right side of life—in your decision for Christ, in your resistance to the tempter, in your choice of Eternal Life. These are the acts and decisions which are blessedly irrevocable and the influence of which will abide till moons shall wax and wane no more.

PARTED FOREVER

To save Jacob from the vengeance of Esau, Rebekah urged her son to flee to Mesopotamia and take refuge in her old home—the home of her brother Laban. There he would be safe from Esau's rage, and safe also from another calamity which Rebekah nobly prayed might be spared her—that he should marry a Canaanite as Esau had done. "Flee thou," said Rebekah, "to Laban my brother to Haran; and tarry with him a few days, until thy brother's fury turn away; until thy brother's anger turn away from thee, and he forget that which thou hast done to him: then I will send, and fetch thee from thence: why should I be deprived also of you both in one day?"

Yonder is Jacob, starting on his long journey to Mesopotamia with his staff and his bundle over his shoulder. Take a last, long look, Rebekah, for it is not for "a few days" only, as you fondly suppose, but for thirty years and more. Never again, Rebekah, wilt thou see the face of that loved son. Yonder he goes. Now he stops, and turning, looks back at the encampment of Isaac, and waves to his mother, who waves back to him. Now his form is lost on the distant horizon. Morning will dawn again about your black tents, Rebekah. The tinkle of the goats' bells and the bleating of the sheep will be heard tomorrow as of old. The sun will rise in splendor and in splendor go down again, and when night comes down Orion will stretch his golden band across the heavens and the Pleiades will look down upon the earth; but Jacob thou wilt never see again, for when Jacob returns, Rebekah, thou wilt be sleeping by the side of Isaac and by the side of Abraham and Sarah in Machpelah's lonely cavern.

NEVERTHELESS, A GREAT MOTHER

With all her faults Rebekah was a great woman and a great mother. Her consuming ambition was that Jacob should fulfill the destiny that was marked out for him at his birth when the Lord said the elder should serve the younger. It was not for herself, but for him, for his future and for the glory of the promise given to Abraham, that Rebekah acted. If she fell into guile and deception, her motive was high. Like Salome, the mother of James and John, who asked for seats at the right hand and left hand of Christ in glory for her two sons, Rebekah asked a high spiritual destiny for her son. Cardinal Vaughan used to say that his mother never once asked a temporal blessing for her many children, but always that they might stand high with God. Mothers, what kind of blessings do you ask for your sons and daughters? Do you pray first of all, above all else, that they should be redeemed men and women, the children of God?

"WILT THOU GO?"

Always, when we think of Rebekah, this is the refrain that comes back to us: "Wilt thou go with this man?" That was what Eliezer and her family said to her—"Wilt thou go with this man?" But I think now of another messenger who comes—none other than God's Holy Spirit—and of another Man with whom you are invited to go—the Man of Galilee, the One altogether lovely. The Holy Spirit asks you, "Wilt thou go with this man?" "His left hand is under your head, and his right hand doth embrace you." Hear the voice of your Beloved. You need his affection. You need his protection. You need his kindness and his strength. Are you going through life without Christ? If you choose him, he will never leave you nor forsake you. Sorrows, failures, trials, and tribulations will come upon you. Youth and its beauty and its transient charms will pass. But he will love you with an everlasting love. In every condition and circumstance and every hour of life, and in the rolling years of eternity you will prove his sovereign, eternal, unchangeable love. Wilt thou go with this Man?

IX

THE WOMAN WHO MARRIED THE RIGHT MAN

> "And they seemed unto him but a few days, for the love he had to her."
>
> GENESIS 29:20

WHERE IS THERE A RECORD THAT SURPASSES THAT? For the love which he bore to Rachel, seven years seemed to Jacob but a few days. Other men would have become discouraged and given it up. Others would have been taken with another face, fallen in love with another woman. Others would have said, "There are as good fish in the sea as ever came out of it," and would have fished elsewhere. But not Jacob. He was not that kind. Strange co-mixture of the heavenly and the earthly, the spiritual and the sensual, yet Jacob had that quality which lifted him above mankind. He had a divine persistence and perseverance. We see it that night by the fords of the Jabbok, when he wrestled with his mysterious adversary until the breaking of the day, and would not let him go until he blessed him. Here Jacob wrestles for seven years with the Angel of Love and will not let him go until he blesses him.

The Bible is first in everything: first in history,

first in biography, first in philosophy, first in poetry, first in prophecy. Therefore it is not strange that it is first also in love. And here is the greatest lover of the Bible. Jacob outsoars all the great lovers of history—Hero and Leander, Dante and Beatrice, Abélard and Héloïse. Seven years seemed to him but a few days while he waited for Rachel. Two thousand five hundred and fifty-five days seemed like little more than a day with Jacob for the love he had to Rachel!

If Thomas Moore's beautiful song had been written at that time, when Jacob kissed Rachel by that old well of Mesopotamia—or at any other time in their long association, clear down to their parting for this life, not far from the gates of Bethlehem— I am sure that is the song Jacob would have sung to Rachel:

Believe me, if all those endearing young charms,
    Which I gaze on so fondly today,
Were to change by tomorrow, and fleet in my arms,
    Like fairy-gifts fading away,
Thou wouldst still be ador'd, as this moment thou art,
    Let thy loveliness fade as it will,
And around the dear ruin each wish of my heart
    Wound entwine itself verdantly still.

Coleridge once remarked of Jacob, "No one could love like that and be wholly bad." When Rachel married Jacob she married the right man.

This, too, is a story which commences at a Meso-potamian well. Yonder comes Jacob, with his bundle and staff over his shoulder. He had fled from the wrath of his brother Esau, whom he had basely cheated out of Isaac's blessing. On the way he had a visit with the angels at Bethel, when he saw the ladder which stretched from heaven to earth with the angels of God ascending and descending, and heard the promise that God would be with him wher-ever he went and would bring him again unto his father's house.

When he reached the well, Jacob revealed the aggressiveness of his character—and, indeed, of his race—by proceeding to give orders and instruc-tions to the shepherds, telling them to water the sheep and then feed them. They told him they would not water the sheep or feed them until the stone was rolled away from the mouth of the well. While he was talking with them, Rachel came to the well with her father's sheep. That was the turning point in Jacob's life and in Rachel's life. Providence brought them together at that well, where they drank of one single cup and never separated again until death parted them.

Stirred and animated by the beauty of Rachel, Jacob hurried to roll away the stone from the mouth of the well. The women who came to the sepulcher on the morning of the Resurrection wondered who would roll away the stone from the door of the sepulcher for them, but an angel had already done that. As Rachel came to that well on that summer day, and saw the shepherds and others standing about it, no doubt she too wondered who would roll away the stone from the mouth of the well for her. But Jacob was there, appointed of God from all eternity to do that very work for Rachel. And when he had rolled away the stone, he "kissed Rachel, and lifted up his voice, and wept."

Why did he weep? If he wept, why did he kiss her? And if he kissed her, why did he weep? Jacob himself would have to tell you that. Yet how true it is in life; kisses and tears come close together. The tears of dew are on the flower at morning, when the sun kisses its face. Kisses and tears, tears and kisses, sorrow and joy, joy and sorrow, the brightness of life and the mytery of life—these follow one another in swift, unchanging succession.

Laban, Rachel's father, who had let Rebekah go to be the wife of Isaac without making anything out of it, was determined this time to profit out of the love that Jacob had for his beautiful daughter Rachel. So he made the hard bargain that Jacob was to serve him seven years for the hand of Rachel. Seven years was a long time—what they call a complete cycle of life, in which all the particles of our bodies change; so that physically, as they tell us, a new man, a new woman, emerges. Think of all the things that have happened to you in seven years—changes in your family, changes in the world, changes in your body, changes in your heart. But it did not seem a long time to Jacob. It seemed but a few days for the love which he had to her. Perhaps they met sometimes, without the grasping Laban's knowing it, at that old well, where they sat together and looked down into the water and, seeing the star reflected there, read together their common destiny. But, whether they did or not, the seven years passed quickly by for the infatuated Jacob.

There is the first reason why Rachel married the right man. She married a man who was capable of deep and tender and abiding romance and affection.

At length comes round the marriage day. The seven years' labor and apprenticeship are over. Now Jacob, before all the people of the village, who have gathered from far and near for the festivities, comes to claim his bride. The words of mutual avowal are spoken, the gifts are exchanged, and then Jacob leads Rachel to his tent. But when she unveils herself, lo, it is not Rachel—not the woman he loved, and for whom he had waited seven years—but the ill-favored and cross-eyed Leah! Laban had played a wretched trick on Jacob and had palmed off on him the older and unattractive daughter.

It is hard to tell from the narrative whether, after

a week had passed, Jacob was permitted to marry Rachel also, and then serve another seven years for her, or whether he must wait the fourteen years. But whether he married her then, or at the end of the second period, he served and labored for her fourteen years; and I doubt not that at the end of the second seven years he would have said what he said at the end of the first seven years—that they seemed to him but a few days. Yes, love shortens the day. Love shortens the journey. Love lifts the burden. Love lights up the pathway. With love all things are possible; and long waiting passes quickly where love holds the torch and shows the way.

Why did Jacob not resent the gross fraud of Laban? Why did he not fell Laban to the ground with his shepherd's staff? I suppose one reason was that Jacob felt that he was being punished for his own deception. It is written that "he that doeth wrong shall receive for the wrong that he hath done." Sometimes sin is not only punished, but punished in kind. Here we have an instance of that. Jacob had deceived and cheated his father and his brother. Now he in turn is deceived and cheated by Laban. That, no doubt, was one reason why Jacob made no protest. His conscience said to him, "Thou art the man."

The home life of Rachel was at first unhappy. It was unhappy, too, for Leah—wretchedly unhappy, for she knew that Rachel had Jacob's love. Leah had six children, but Rachel had none. Deep pathos there is in that utterance of Leah when her first child was born. She called his name Reuben, "for," she said, "surely the Lord hath looked on my affliction. Now, therefore, my husband will love me." Many a young wife and mother has fondly, but vainly, uttered that same hope and prayer. "Now that our child is born, now will my husband love me." "Now that we have a child, my husband will treat me kindly." "Now that we have a child he will stop drinking." "Now that we have a child he will go to church with me." Beautiful, but sad, because ofttimes a fruitless hope and prayer.

Leah had six children, but Rachel had none. Every time she heard one of Leah's children cry in the neighboring tent it cut her to the heart with envy and grief and self-reproach. The only time that even the shadow of a cloud came between Jacob and Rachel was when Rachel said to him, in her distress, "Give me children, or else I die." And Jacob exclaimed, "Am I in God's stead, who hath withheld from thee the fruit of the womb?"

At length the prayer and the cry of Rachel were answered, and Joseph was born to her. That was a child worth waiting for! Then the long years that Rachel had waited for Joseph seemed to her but a few days, as did the years that Jacob had waited for Rachel. In the mystery of maternity and childhood, all the sorrows and disappointments of her life were forgotten. Only such lovers could have produced such a child—that wonderful Joseph, in many respects the prince of all the characters of the Old Testament, and certainly the most Christlike among them; Christian in spirit and forgiveness beyond his time.

One day Jacob's black tents were struck. He was migrating westward again and separating himself from Laban. His two wives, Leah and Rachel, with the seven children, and the other children whom he had by their maids, and all their attendants, started with him on the long trek to the land of Canaan; for God had spoken to Jacob and told him to come back to his father's country. On the way Jacob received an alarming message. Esau his brother was marching to meet him with four hundred armed men! Esau! That was the man of all men whom Jacob wished to forget—Esau whom he had cheated, Esau whom he had wronged. Twenty years had passed since that base deception; but now the infamy and sin of Jacob come back to him with unchanged freshness. How mysterious and how strange is the vitality of sin. Twenty years have come and gone, but Jacob's heart sinks within him as he hears that Esau his brother is marching toward him and four hundred armed men with him. Those tidings stirred the pool of conscience within the breast of Jacob. Sin is one traveler who never changes and never grows old.

That night, after he passed his families and flocks and herds over ahead of him, Jacob, held by some mysterious power, tarried on the other side of the Jabbok. "And Jacob was left alone; and there wrestled a man with him until the breaking of the day." Mysterious, unaccountable, indescribable conflict! The angel wrestling with Jacob! Jacob wrestling with the angel! Who, until we meet that angel and Jacob himself in heaven, will be able to tell us all that that struggle meant? But as to the results, there is nothing mysterious. Jacob emerged from that battle with the angel a changed man with a new name. He was no longer Jacob, the Supplanter; but Israel, one who had power with God.

And there is another reason why Rachel married the right man. She married a man upon whose life was the touch of God. At least once in his life every man has one close encounter with God, and in that night and in that encounter great things are possible for the soul. Out of the midnight struggle men learn that God is love and that he smites only to bless. How beautifully that is put in Charles Wesley's great hymn, one of the best commentaries on that mysterious battle.

Come, O thou Traveler unknown,
　Whom still I hold, but cannot see;
My company before is gone,
　And I am left alone with thee.
With thee all night I mean to stay,
And wrestle till the break of day.

I need not tell thee who I am,
　My sin and misery declare;
Thyself hast called me by my name—
　Look on thy hands, and read it there:
But who, I ask thee, who art thou?
Tell me thy name, and tell me now.

Yield to me now, for I am weak,
　But confident in self-despair;
Speak to my heart, in blessing speak;
　Be conquered by my instant prayer:
Speak, or thou never hence shalt move,
And tell me if thy name be Love.

'Tis Love! 'Tis Love! Thou diedst for me!
　I hear thy whisper in my heart;
The morning breaks, the shadows flee;
　Pure, universal Love thou art:
To me, to all, thy mercies move;
Thy nature and thy name is Love.

On that critical night, when his whole future
seemed at stake, Jacob took great precautions for
the safety of the beloved Rachel. Both Jacob's
father and his grandfather, Isaac and Abraham,

when they felt that their lives were in danger, had practiced a cowardly stratagem, passing their wives off as their sisters in order that they might protect themselves, and not caring what happened to the honor of Rebekah and Sarah. But not so Jacob! With all his many gross faults, and occasional sensuality, Jacob would never have done that. No! Rachel was the apple of his eye. In order to protect her, he put the servants with their flocks and herds in advance; and after them Leah and her maids, and their children and servants; and then, furthest in the rear—furthest away from the point of danger— he put the beloved Rachel and Joseph. There is another reason why Rachel married the right man: he was a man who had deep and tender and affectionate solicitude for her welfare.

When Jacob returned to Canaan, instead of going to Bethel to worship, as there twenty years before he had vowed to do, he settled down in the lush pastures of Shechem, where his family sank into idolatry. There Jacob forgot all about Bethel, and if at times there came a fleeting vision of a youth dreaming at Bethel, of a ladder reaching unto heaven, and the angels ascending and descending, he quickly dismissed such unearthly things and fell to counting his sheep and cattle. But one day God spoke to him and said, "Arise, go up to Bethel, and dwell there; and make there an altar unto God, that appeared unto thee when thou fleddest from the face of Esau thy brother."

So God calls men back to their better selves. So God calls men back to the early dreams and the holy aspirations of their lives. The first thing that Jacob did was to bury the idols that his family had accumulated; for he knew that he could not take them with him to Bethel and find God again. Then, with Rachel and Joseph, and all his family, he set out once more for Bethel. He found the stone upon which his head had rested that night, set it up for a pillar, and knelt down and worshiped the God who had appeared unto him there. And God appeared again unto Jacob and blessed him. I can imagine how, as they sat together there on the starlit desert, Jacob told Rachel of the events of that wonderful night.

And there is another reason why Rachel married the right man: he was a man who, in his best moments, could see more than sheep and cattle, and black tents, and the things of this world. He was a man who could see ladders reaching to heaven and the angels of God ascending and descending.

At length the fairest and most sacred friendships and associations of life come to the parting of the ways. Yes; that was prophesied at the very beginning—there at the well in Mesopotamia, when, after he had drawn water for his sheep, Jacob kissed

Rachel and lifted up his voice and wept. Kisses and tears! Prophetic kisses! Prophetic tears! And here we find them—kisses and tears—close together again, when Jacob and Rachel are parted. They were journeying together from Bethel; and, like another mother of Joseph's own line and descent centuries afterward, when they got almost to Bethlehem, Rachel's great hour came upon her and she went down again into the valley of motherhood. This time she did not emerge from that valley; and, in her plaintive grief, the son that she was leaving behind her she called "Benoni"—"the son of my sorrow." But brokenhearted Jacob could not bear to think of that, and called him "Benjamin"—"the son of my right hand." For the last time Jacob looked on that beautiful face—the face that had won him there at the well when first he saw her. With Jacob it had been love at first sight—and second sight, third sight, and all through the years, down to the very end.

In order to memorialize and perpetuate his grief, Jacob reared a tomb and monument to the memory of Rachel; and there you can still see it, not far from the gates of Bethlehem. But Rachel's real tomb was in Jacob's heart. She lived again, too, in those two sons, Joseph and Benjamin. Jacob thought he had drunk deep enough of sorrow's cup; but there was another bitter draught for him when his sons came home one day and told him that

Joseph was dead—Joseph, whose every look and whose beautiful life mirrored for Jacob the face and the life of the mother Rachel. But out of that sorrow Jacob was at length delivered, when he saw the chariots of Pharaoh and knew that Joseph still lived.

Now the old patriarch is dying down in Egypt. He gathers his sons and grandsons about him, and with that energy of soul which never forsook him, pronounces a blessing upon them one by one. Just before Joseph's children, Ephraim and Manasseh, are brought unto him, the old man's mind wanders back to Rachel, and this is what he says: "Rachel died by me in the land of Canaan in the way when yet there was but little way to come unto Ephrath; and I buried her there in the way of Ephrath; the same is Bethlehem."

So with his latest breath Jacob speaks of Rachel. It makes one think of that stern old American soldier and president, Andrew Jackson, sitting in his beautiful home, the Hermitage, near Nashville, with all the storms of his turbulent life behind him, and the harbor lights of eternity beginning to flash for him, in one hand holding the Bible, and in the other the miniature of his own Rachel—the beloved Rachel who for him was next to the Bible itself. And there is another reason why Rachel married the right man: she married a man who tenderly and reverently cherished her memory long after she was in her grave.

So life goes on—its pilgrimages, its flights, its fears, its angelic visions, its ladders reaching to heaven, its altars, its apostasies, its illusions, its trials, its hardships, its sorrows—and yet all made tolerable by the light of love. And what is this love that Jacob had for Rachel but the shadow of a greater and deeper love? With a word about that love, I now conclude.

Jacob became Israel, a prince of God; and it was this prince of God who loved Rachel to the end. But the One who loves you is none other than the Prince of Heaven himself. Jacob loved Rachel for seven years before he took her as his wife, and then loved her clear down to the end of her life. But Christ has loved you from before the foundation of the world. "I have loved thee," he says, "with an everlasting love." Jacob toiled hard for Rachel seven years; but this thy Lover toiled and suffered for thee on the Cross. Jacob endured the heat of the day and the cool of the night through all those seven years for the love which he had to Rachel. But your Eternal Lover endured the pain and despised the shame on the cursed Tree for you. They taunted him on the Cross, and said to him, "If thou be the Son of God, come down from the cross." But he would not come down, for he was thinking of you and the salvation of your soul. Therefore he could not, and would not, come down from the Cross.

Will you take now his redeeming love? You will need that wonderful love for life—for all its trials and sorrows, and battles, and temptations, and hard and lonely places. You will need that love in the hour of death. You will need it for the Day of Judgment. He will never leave you nor ever forsake you. Jacob had to part from Rachel, there near the gates of Bethlehem; but your Eternal Lover will never leave you and never forsake you. Will you take him now, and rejoice forever and ever in his sovereign, unchangeable, unspeakable Love?

X

THE WOMAN WHO HAD FIVE HUS-
BANDS—AND ONE WHO WAS NOT

> "Thou hast had five husbands; and he
> whom thou now hast is not thy husband."
> JOHN 4:18

THIS IS ANOTHER OF THOSE BEAUTIFUL AND MEM-
orable scenes at the wells of the Bible. Only this
time it is not Moses wooing Zipporah at her father's
well in the desert, nor Eliezer wooing Rebekah for
Isaac at the well of Mesopotamia, nor Jacob wooing
Rachel by the well of Haran; but Christ himself,
the Eternal Lover, wooing the soul of a woman who
was a sinner.

This is one of the greatest scenes in the Bible.
So clearly and fully is it related by John—who must
have been greatly impressed by it, since he gives so
much space to it—that it is easy to follow and envisage after the lapse of all these centuries. It
came early in the ministry of our Lord; and yet
here are some of the sublimest profundities of his
teachings.

The Pharisees were saying that Jesus was baptizing more people than John. Not wishing to
reflect in any way upon his great forerunner, Jesus

—who, himself, was not baptizing at all, but his disciples—left Judea to go to Galilee. "And," John says, "he must needs go through Samaria." Because of the ancient feud between the Jews and the Samaritans, no orthodox Jew would pass through Samaria if he could help it. The Samaritans were not real Jews, but descendants of Assyrians who had been colonized in Samaria after the conquest of that kingdom by the Assyrians. These colonists had been instructed by a priest of Israel sent to them from the captives in Assyria. The result was a dual worship which combined the heathen idolatries with the worship of the true God. Their sacred mountain was Gerizim, where they built a temple. This was why the Jews had no dealings with the Samaritans.

But John says that Jesus "must needs go through Samaria" on his way to Galilee. The orthodox Jew, rather than do that, would cross the Jordan twice—into Perea and then back again—and reach Galilee by that roundabout journey. But Jesus went through Samaria. It is evident from what follows that he did so because he was convinced that there were those in Samaria to whom he could minister. Somewhere in that land and among those ostracized people, there was a soul that was waiting for him. Thus it was that on his journey he came to Sychar, the ancient Shechem where Abraham had dwelt, and Jacob also.

In the summer of 1931, traveling in the other direction—that is, coming from Galilee to Judea and Jerusalem—I left Tiberias, passed along the eastern shore of the Lake of Galilee to Capernaum, and then, leaving the Sea of Galilee, went to Cana, where Jesus turned water into wine; from there to Nazareth; then across the plain of Esdraelon to the ruins of Jezreel, where the apostate Ahab and the ferocious Jezebel had their palace. From there I crossed the plains of Dothan, where the sons of Jacob were tending their flocks that morning when they lifted up their eyes and saw Joseph in the distance with his coat of many colors. From Dothan I continued to Sebaste, high up on the top of a mountain, and the site of Samaria, the capital of the northern kingdom of Israel, with the supposed graves of Elisha, Obadiah, and John the Baptist. There you can see the ruins of Herod's palace, where Salome danced before Herod and his lords. Continuing my journey, I came to Nablus, one of the most fanatical of the Arab towns, on the site of the ancient Shechem.

It was to this same place that Jesus came on his journey to Galilee. You can see, rising on either side of the valley, Mount Gerizim, where Joshua stationed half the people to pronounce the blessings, and across from it, Mount Ebal, where he stationed half the people to pronounce the curses. Down in the valley, surrounded by a square wall, is the ancient well of Jacob. When a man plants a tree or digs a well he blesses mankind for generations to come. When the awards and honorable mentions are given out in Heaven, I expect to see well-diggers and tree-planters stand much higher on the list than many a poet and painter and speaker and inventor and soldier. The well is one hundred and five feet deep and nine feet in diameter. The priest of the little Greek church lowered the vessel far down into the well, where we heard it strike the water, and presently he drew it up again, "dripping with coolness." As I drank of that pure water, the centuries vanished, and I saw Christ sitting on the very curb of the well where I was sitting, and asking the woman of Samaria for a drink of water.

John says that Jesus, "being wearied with his journey, sat thus on the well." The sun was just as hot then and the roads were just as hard then as they are today in that part of the world. Jesus was tired; just as I was tired, when I sat thus on the well and asked for a drink. Only he was much more tired, because he had come all the way from Judaea on foot. Here we have the Weary Christ. That makes you understand how often Jesus must have been weary on those long journeys of his. But from what followed we see that, weary as he was, he was not too weary to work for God, and not too weary to forget his own fatigue and his own hunger and thirst that he might save a soul. How easily we excuse ourselves from labor for the church and for Christ on the ground that we are tired and weary. But Christ was never too weary to help a soul. I think it was Wesley—or was it Whitefield? —who said, "Lord, I am weary in thy work, but not of it."

Jesus dismissed the disciples to go to the village of Sychar and buy bread. The fact that he sent all the disciples away arouses our interest. Was there something in Christ's mind that John did not tell us here—the conviction, the premonition, that he was to meet this woman? There Christ sits alone by the well. It is one of the few times that we see Christ by himself. He was alone at the beginning of his ministry, when he was tempted of the devil in the wilderness; and alone when he prayed on the mountain top; and alone in the Garden of Gethsemane. There is something very moving and appealing about this incident in the life of our Lord, as we see him sitting there all by himself, looking down into that deep well.

Presently Jesus hears the sound of sandals on the stony pathway. Looking up, he sees a woman who has come out from Sychar with a waterpot on her shoulder. Why had she come at that hot hour of the day—the sixth hour? Why had she come alone?

In that land you can still see the women going out in groups to draw water at the early morning hour, or at the evening hour, talking gaily with one another. But this woman came alone, and at the hottest hour of the day. Perhaps it was that she might avoid the sneers and taunts of the other women, who knew her past, and her present.

From what is said, we gather that this woman was not old, and yet was not young—somewhere in that border land between youth and middle age. In her face are lingering traces of a departed beauty, and from her conversation it is evident that she has a quick, engaging, and pleasing mind. It is not hard to understand how she charmed so many lovers. But now all that is past. She had given herself to passion, and now the fires of passion have burned themselves out in her. Despised by her neighbors, she comes to the well alone, not weary in body like Christ, but weary and depressed in spirit.

Seeing her, Jesus said, "Give me to drink." There is nothing in John's story to indicate that the woman was in any way discourteous to Christ, or that she intended to refuse him a drink. But she knew at once, by his appearance, that he was a Jew; and she expressed her surprise that he should deign to talk with a Samaritan woman—and still more, to make a request of her. There was perhaps more in that request of Christ's than the woman understood.

In his agony on the cross Christ cried, "I thirst!" And it was more than a thirst for water. It was a thirst for souls. So when he asked this woman for a drink, it was drink divine, too, that he wanted. He was athirst for a soul.

The woman, whose way of talking catches and pleases us today just as it must have pleased Jesus, said to him, "How is it that thou, being a Jew, askest drink of me, which am a woman of Samaria?" Jesus did not enter into the merits of that ancient dispute between the Jews and the Samaritans, or say why he had disregarded the prejudice of his race. Instead of that, he told her of a real and present opportunity. How eagerly he reached out after this woman's soul! He said to her: "If thou knewest the gift of God, and who it is that saith unto thee, Give me to drink; thou wouldest have asked of him, and he would have given thee living water." It is as if he had said, "Woman, I have asked you for a drink of water; but if you only knew who I am, and what I can do for you, you would ask of me, and I would give you living water."

Living water! How much of the meaning of Jesus did the woman grasp? Probably very little of what you and I understand today. And yet it is clear that in the soul of this woman—as, conscious or unconscious, in the soul of everyone—there was a thirst after something higher and better. Christ had at least aroused her curiosity. "Who is this," she thought—"this stranger who tells me that I ought to ask a drink of him; and that if I did, he would give me living water? And what is living water?" So in her perplexity, and now with the greatest respect she said, "Sir, thou hast nothing to draw with, and the well is deep: from whence then hast thou that living water? Art thou greater than our father Jacob, which gave us the well, and drank thereof himself, and his children, and his cattle?" In other words, "Have you better water that Jacob had, better water than this well where the generations of men and women have slaked their thirst?"

Then came that great answer of Jesus. His was not only a deeper well, and the water in it better than any other water, but so much better that one drink of it quenches thirst forever; and that water, once tasted, becomes a well of water springing up unto Eternal Life. Jesus said, "Whosoever drinketh of this water shall thirst again: but whosoever drinketh of the water that I shall give him shall never thirst; but the water that I shall give him shall be in him a well of water springing up into everlasting life."

Here again we cannot say how much the woman understood of what Christ was saying. Certainly, he had stirred her soul with a desire for something more than just water. The interview had started by Jesus making a request of the woman. Now she makes a request of him. "Whatever he means," she thought to herself, "he looks and speaks as if he could make good what he says. At least he can relieve me of this long, hard journey; toiling from here up to the village on the hillside with this water-pot on my shoulder." So she said, "Sir, give me this water, that I thirst not, neither come hither to draw."

Then came the startling and, to her, amazing reply of Jesus. "Go, call thy husband."

"My husband! What has that to do with it?" she must have thought to herself. And likewise, at the first reading, we think today, for it seems altogether irrelevant, an inappropriate inconsequence. But the purpose of Christ was to appeal to the woman's sense of sin, and show her that she could not drink—as no one can—of the Living Water until she had repented. Not imagining that Jesus had any real knowledge about her history and her life, and wondering why he had asked about her husband, she said—what was not true in the sense that she meant it—"I have no husband."

Then Jesus, who had complete knowledge of the woman's past and her history, said to her, "Thou hast well said, I have no husband: for thou hast had five husbands; and he whom thou now hast is not thy husband; in that saidst thou truly." She had had five husbands, now either dead or separated from her, and at present was living in sin with a man who was not her husband.

Silent for the moment, subdued and awed by this marvelous insight into her life, the woman said, "Sir, I perceive that thou art a prophet." She was certain now of what she had felt all through this remarkable interview—that she was dealing with no ordinary man.

But she now had such reverence and respect for him that she felt ashamed and abashed that he should know of her unworthy life, and in the most natural way sought to turn the discussion away from herself to a matter of race and theological dispute. From where she was sitting she could see the grim outlines of Mount Gerizim. That suggested to her a way of escape from the probing of Jesus. So she said, pointing to the mount where the Samaritans had their temple, "Our fathers worshipped in this mountain; and ye say, that in Jerusalem is the place where men ought to worship." In other words, "The theologians and the doctors differ. I should like to know what you think on the subject." And Jesus, accommodating himself for the moment to this subject, and indulging the woman, did turn aside to discuss that question. He said the Jews were right. They had the true religion. The Samaritans worshiped they knew not what. Salvation is of the Jews. "But," he added, "the hour cometh,

and now is, when the true worshippers shall worship
the Father in spirit and in truth: for the Father
seeketh such to worship him. God is a Spirit: and
they that worship him must worship him in spirit
and in truth." Thus he tells her that the true approach to God is not now by way of Mount Gerizim,
nor Mount Zion, but by repentance and faith, and
a heart cleansed of sin.

To this the woman answered, no doubt with something of a sigh, and greatly stirred in her heart, and
still perplexed in her mind, "I know that Messias
cometh, which is called Christ: when he is come, he
will tell us all things"; that is, he will settle all these
disputes and we shall all worship him. Then said
Jesus, "I that speak unto thee am he!" Now the
woman understood his power to search her heart.
Now she understood why he could offer her the
Water of Life. The stranger who sat on the curb
of the well of Jacob, looking into her face, was
the Messiah of Israel!

Just at that moment the disciples returned from
Sychar, whither they had gone to buy bread. They
looked with astonishment upon their Master engaged
in conversation with this solitary woman. Yet there
was a light in his face—and, I am sure, a light in her
face—which silenced every question that was in their
minds. Seeing them, the woman hastily withdrew,
forgetting her waterpot and leaving it behind her as

she went back to the city. There she said to the men of Sychar, "Come, see a man, which told me all things that ever I did: is not this the Christ?" Then they went out—probably with her again—to the well and talked with Jesus. Many of them believed on Jesus because of what the woman had told them about him, and what she testified, saying, "He told me all that ever I did." They besought him to remain in their city, and he accepted their invitation and stayed for two days; during that period many more believed on him because of his own word. They said to the woman of Samaria, "Now we believe, not because of thy saying: for we have heard him ourselves, and know that this is indeed the Christ, the Saviour of the world."

But before Jesus accepted their invitation and came to the city with them, he spoke a great word there to his disciples at the well. They brought out their bread and said, "Master, eat." But Jesus had forgotten all about his hunger and his thirst. He said, "I have meat to eat that ye know not of." And following that came this great word: "Lift up your eyes, and look on the fields; for they are white already to harvest. And he that reapeth receiveth wages, and gathereth fruit unto life eternal." What he meant was that all about them, even there in despised Samaria, there were souls ready to be won for the Kingdom of God.

There are three great truths that we taste here at this well of Samaria, as we drink of its waters.

ONLY CHRIST CAN SATISFY THE SOUL

The first is, that Christ alone can satisfy the thirst of an immortal soul. Jesus said, "Whosoever drinketh of this water shall thirst again." Men have experimented with every well of this world. They have drunk of the water of power, the water of fame, the water of knowledge, the water of riches, and the water of sensual pleasure—but only to thirst again. When you think of it, how few faces there are, as you see them on the street, or anywhere else, that show complete content and satisfaction. No; they are all thirsting, consciously or unconsciously, for something higher. God hath put eternity in the heart, and he alone can satisfy that thirst.

Jesus said, "The water that I shall give him shall be in him a well of water"; that is, henceforth, he does not depend upon external things, but depends upon that well of water within himself. All parts of the world have their fables and myths about fountains and wells which had the power to bestow eternal youth and to satisfy man's every desire. But here is the only well and the only water which can do that.

Some years ago, driving up the Syrian coast between Tripoli and Antioch, I came to the enormous

Crusaders' stronghold, the Krak des Chevaliers, an immense world of stone where the Crusaders defended themselves against the Moslems. In the very heart and center of that colossal citadel and fortress was the ancient well into which the caretaker let down his vessel and drew water for us. All the old castles had their own well upon which they could depend when cut off from the rest of the world. When the world fails you, or turns against you, have you a well within you—a well of faith in Christ, springing up into Eternal Life?

THE DIVINE IN EVERY SOUL

The second truth that we drink out of this well of Jacob is this: There is a beauty and priceless value in every soul. How the Bible likes to declare and illustrate that, and never more beautifully than here. Here was this woman with her shady past, her five husbands, and her present companion in sin; and yet of all the women in Samaria at that time, this is the one for whom Christ was looking. In her he found the pearl of great price.

> Down in the human heart
> Crushed by the tempter;
> Feelings lie buried that grace can restore:
> Touched by a loving heart,
> Wakened by kindness,
> Chords that were broken will vibrate once more.[1]

[1] Fanny J. Crosby.

[165]

THE PASSING OPPORTUNITY

The third and last important truth that we taste in the water out of this old well is the importance and the value of the moment. This was a wayside chance. The woman almost missed it; but through the goodness of Christ she did ask for and did receive the Water of Life. When, in answer to Jesus' request for a drink, she said, "How is it that thou, being a Jew, askest drink of me, who am a woman of Samaria?" Jesus replied, in all the eagerness of his soul, "If thou knewest the gift of God, and who it is that saith to thee, Give me to drink; thou wouldest have asked of him, and he would have given thee living water." She did know before that interview was over; and she did ask of him, and did receive the Living Water.

Yet how solemn are those words of Christ, "If thou knewest the gift of God"! Oh, how oblivious we often are to our opportunity! The Great Traveler passes our way; and too often as he goes by the soul does not ask of him and does not receive. How nearly this woman missed the gift of Eternal Life. Lord, open our eyes to the sacredness of the divine opportunity.

Christ said to this woman, "If thou knewest." He used the present tense, for he meant, "If thou wilt, thou canst know who I am and what I can give to thee, and thou canst ask of me, and I will give it thee." But there was another and sadder occasion when Jesus used this same phrase, but this time in the past tense; not, "If *thou knewest*," but, alas, "If thou *hadst* known!" That is what he said to the people of Jerusalem when he saw the city and wept over it. "If thou *hadst* known, even thou, at least in this thy day, the things which belong unto thy peace! but now they are hid from thine eyes, ... because thou knewest not the time of thy visitation."

The time of thy visitation! God give you grace to know that. The Holy Spirit is speaking to you, I am sure. Oh, do not turn away! If thou knewest the gift of God, and who it is for whom God's Holy Spirit speaks, thou wouldst ask of him. You may be even now on the edge of the supreme moment of your life. If thou *knewest!* Before Christ must say, "If thou *hadst* known," ask now, and thou shalt receive Eternal Life.

XI

THE WOMAN WHO LOST AND FOUND
LIFE'S GREATEST TREASURE

"Thou shalt embrace a son."

II KINGS 4:16

"He sat on her knees till noon, and then died."

II KINGS 4:20

"Take up thy son."

II KINGS 4:36

THERE YOU HAVE IT! THERE IS THE WOMAN WHO got, lost, and got again, life's greatest gift. What greater gift is there than a son? What greater loss than to lose a son, and what greater joy than to get him back again?

Between the getting, the losing, and the finding again of that son, lies one of the great stories of the Bible, and the history of one of the Bible's greatest women. Near the present ruins of Jezreel, in the valley of Esdraelon, is a little village called Sulem, standing on the site of the ancient town of Shunem. In this town there lived one who was spoken of as "a great woman." As we shall see, she was great in other ways—great in her faith, great in her courage, great in her kindness and hospitality; but what is meant here, when she is called a great woman, is that she was a woman of prominence, of high standing, and of wealth. Little is said of her husband, for the woman seems to have been the chief partner in

[168]

this marriage. All persons of note who came through that town were entertained at her home.

Elisha happened to pass that way on one of his journeys through the land, and was invited to eat bread in this woman's house. They were taken with Elisha and he with them, and thus it came about that whenever he passed that way he stayed in their home. One day, after Elisha had been their guest and had departed on his journey, the woman said to her husband, "Behold now, I perceive that this is an holy man of God, which passeth by us continually." A splendid description that, of a godly, consecrated, and industrious minister of the Gospel—"an holy man of God, which passeth by us continually." "Let us," the woman said to her husband, "make a little chamber on the wall; and let us set for him there a bed, and a table, and a stool, and a candlestick: and it shall be, when he cometh to us, that he shall turn in thither." The woman's husband gave ready consent to her proposal. The stonemasons and the carpenters were called in, and before many months had passed the addition to the house was completed; and either on the flat roof of the house, or extending from its wall, there was a separate apartment for Elisha, with a private entrance. It was spoken of as "the prophet's chamber"; and down to this day that phrase is used to describe the room in the house where the visiting minister is entertained. In old Alexander Hall at Princeton that is what they call the guest chamber—the "Prophet's Chamber."

One day, while Elisha was resting from his journeys in this prophet's chamber, he was moved to do something which would show his gratitude for this woman's kindness and hospitality. He told his servant, Gehazi, to call the woman to his apartment. When she stood before him, he said, "Behold, thou hast been careful for us with all this care; what is to be done for thee? wouldest thou be spoken for to the king, or to the captain of the host?" Elisha was a man of power in the kingdom, and his word went a long way with the king and with the captain of the host. But here was a woman who was satisfied with her lot. She told Elisha that there was nothing she desired him to do for her, saying, "I dwell among mine own people."

In consultation with Gehazi afterward, Elisha wondered what could be done as a token of gratitude to this woman. Then Gehazi told him—what the prophet, singularly enough, had not thought of—that since the woman had no child she must greatly desire one. That was true. The woman had wealth; she had social position; she had health; she had high standing in all that part of the country. But she had no child. She would gladly have exchanged her great house which was childless for a peasant's cottage, if only she could hear the ring of a child's voice.

Elisha then told Gahazi to summon the woman. When she came again to his apartment, Elisha said to her, "About this time of the year thou shalt embrace a son." The woman thought that hardly possible, and said, "Nay; thou art a man of God. Thou must not deceive me that way." Elisha answered nothing, but dismissed her.

And so it came to pass. When the year had gone by she gave birth to a child. You can imagine the change the child made in that home. The great woman now became what was greater, and what is greatest in woman—a great mother. The child was tenderly nourished and brought up. By and by he was able to walk a little, and then to talk; and I am sure that, after the name of Jehovah, the first word they taught him to speak was the name of Elisha. When Elisha stopped at the house on his frequent journeys he would call the lad to his chamber and play with him and talk with him. So the happy years went by, full of sunshine and hope and expectation, until the boy was grown; that is, about twelve years of age.

It is harvest time in the fertile valley of Esdraelon. Before the sun is up, from every little village clustering along the sides of the mountains which guard that great valley the men, women, and children are going forth to the fields. In the distance looms the majestic dome of Mount Tabor, rising high above the plain. Every foot of this fertile valley is historic ground. Over yonder is Gilboa, where Saul and his sons fell in battle with the Philistines. Yonder toward Carmel is the battlefield of Kishon, where Deborah and Barak overcame Sisera and the armies of Canaan. And yonder is where Gideon and his three hundred men, with their pitchers and their trumpets and their swords, routed the vast host of the Midianites. But men cannot live on history. Men must have bread; and year after year, century after century, the fertile fields of Esdraelon have been plowed and sowed and reaped, and so they will be plowed and sowed and reaped until the last great battle—the Battle of Armageddon—is fought there.

Now the sun has risen and the men and women and children are hard at work. Grain standing, grain falling like a receding wave of the sea, grain lying flat on the ground, grain gathered by the binders, grain tied together in bundles, grain tossed into the stack. First of all go the reapers with their sharp and gleaming sickles; then the binders; and last of all the widow and the orphan and the stranger, who gather up some of the grain that has been allowed to remain on the ground, according to the old law, "Thou shalt not wholly reap the corners of thy field." What a picture it is!—the stalwart men bending rhythmically to their task, the women picturesque in their blue skirts, yellow waists, and red headdresses.

In this part of the vast harvest field at which we are looking the head man and master is the well-to-do farmer of the town of Shunem. He is a fine, upright figure, with his dark features and his gray beard. And following him about over the field is his little son.

When the Shunammite landlord started for his field that morning his little boy begged to be taken along. The father consented, but only after the boy's mother had charged him to see that the boy was not allowed to be too long in the sun, for the sun burns fiercely in August in that part of the world. It was a big day for the lad when his father consented to take him to the field. He was put astride a donkey; and, full of pride and joy, he followed the reapers and the gleaners into the field.

Busy with his task of supervision in every part of the broad fields, the boy's father forgot about him for a little, and the lad exposed himself too long to the sun as he ran hither and yonder over the fields, and now and then tried to take a hand himself and gather a little bundle of the grain and tie it into a sheaf. But presently he came running to his father, all the joy and pleasure vanished from his countenance, and cried out, "My head! My head!" His father anxiously took him up in his arms and carried him into the shade of the tent that had been pitched for the comfort of the reapers, and he called for one of the women to do what she could for the lad. One ran for water; another opened his tunic and rubbed his chest and his throat. But the boy was nothing better. All that they heard him murmur as he lapsed into unconsciousness was, "My head! My head!" The anxious father then said to one of his servants, "Carry him to his mother! She will know what to do." So the servant carried him back to the village, where his mother held him on her lap and watched over him and prayed over him until noon, when the child died.

The child was dead. No mother's clasp, no mother's cry, no mother's prayer, could reanimate the body of the lad. The child for whom she had waited so long, and who for twelve years had filled her life with heaven on earth, was dead. I know how that woman felt. I never saw her, but I often heard my mother speak of her first-born child. My father went abroad as a student to study divinity in Scotland. There he fell in love with the daughter of a Glasgow manufacturer. He brought his bride to a little community in what was then the frontier in Ohio. In the course of time a child was born—a daughter who filled that home, and filled the parents' hearts, with joy and sunshine. After a year or two, my mother took the child on a visit to her parents in Scotland.

The brothers and sisters in that home had now married and had homes of their own, and the grandfather and grandmother had their hearts so warmed by the advent of this little granddaughter that they persuaded my mother to leave the child with them, with the promise that in the springtime they would come out to America and bring the child with them. Willing to cheer them in their loneliness, my mother left her with them and returned to America. But she never saw the child again. From what she sometimes said, and from sentences in her diary of that year, I know how she felt. And so I know how this great woman of Shunem felt when her son died on her knees. She felt that the light of life had gone out and that she was living in a dark and empty and hollow cavern.

But the woman did not lose her courage and did not lose her faith. This was a child given of God; perhaps the same God who gave the child would give the lad back to her again. It was natural that she should have thought of Elisha. Taking the child in her arms, she went up to Elisha's chamber and laid him on the prophet's bed and closed the door. Then, returning to her own apartment, she called her husband and asked him to have one of the servants prepare a beast for her to ride, and go with her to Mount Carmel, whence the man of God, Elisha, was. Her husband does not seem to have known that the child was dead, and probably thought that it was just some mild summer complaint, for he expressed great surprise that his wife wanted to start off on such a long journey at that time in the afternoon. His wife gave him no explanation except to say that all would be well. Mounting her beast, she told her servant to drive, and go forward, and not to slow up in the riding.

Elisha was sitting in his retreat on the slopes of Mount Carmel, when he saw in the distance the woman riding her beast along the highway. Looking more carefully, he said to Gehazi, "Yonder is that Shunammite woman. Run to her now, Gehazi, and say to her, Is it well with thee? Is it well with thy husband? Is it well with the child?" When Gehazi met her that was the salutation he gave her. The woman answered briefly, "It is well." Either she did not want Gehazi to know what her trouble was, or she had great faith that in the end all would be well.

Not tarrying to talk with Gehazi, she pressed on toward Elisha, and when she came to where he was standing, fell down and clasped him about the feet. To the coarse-grained and insensitive Gehazi this seemed an unwarranted familiarity on the part of the woman with his master; and, laying a rough hand upon her, he started to push her aside. But Elisha rebuked him, and said, "Let her alone; for her soul

[176]

is vexed within her: and the Lord hath hid it from me, and hath not told me."

Then Elisha asked her what her desire was and what her trouble was. The woman said, "Did I desire a son of my lord? did I not say, Do not deceive me?" That was as far as she went. But from the tone of her voice and the distress in her face, Elisha knew what had happened. Either the child was dead or he was desperately ill. For some reason Elisha did not propose to go himself, at first; but, giving his staff of authority to Gehazi he told him to go in all haste back to Shunem and lay the staff upon the face of the child. He was not to stop or salute anyone by the way, for in the East then, and down to this day, a salutation was a much more lengthy thing than it is with us. Gehazi did as he was bidden. He rode in all haste back to Shunem, and, going up into the chamber, laid the staff upon the face of the child. But there was no response. The child did not awaken.

This is perhaps the only account in the Bible of an attempt to work a miracle which was frustrated, unless we consider as such the attempt of the disciples of Christ to heal the boy possessed of the demon, while Christ and the three disciples were on the Mount of Transfiguration. Why did Elisha's staff fail in this instance? Perhaps because it was in the hand of an unworthy and insincere man, a latent

hypocrite. Perhaps because Elisha ought not to have attempted to restore one to life again through another person, or to substitute the activity of Gehazi for his own. But whatever the reason, the staff failed.

When he arrived at the house Elisha went immediately up to the chamber where the lad lay, and going in shut the door and prayed earnestly unto God. Then he lay down upon the child and stretched himself upon him. After a little he arose and opened the door and walked up and down in the hall, or passageway, saying nothing; and over yonder stood the distraught and anxious, and yet believing, mother. Then Elisha went into the chamber again and shut the door and again stretched himself upon the child. This time the child sneezed and opened his eyes. Life had come back! Opening the door, Elisha called Gehazi and said, "Call the Shunammite woman." When she had come he said to her the sweetest words she had ever heard, "Take up thy son." The woman first fell at his feet and bowed herself to the ground in silent thanks, and then, taking up her child, went out.

This great and unforgettable miracle—perhaps the greatest miracle of the Old Testament—because of the beautiful and pathetic circumstances which attended it, is to us a prediction of the power of Christ to restore the dead to life. Eight hundred and eighty years after that woman took up her child, at the village of Nain, just around the shoulder of the hill from this village of Shunem, Jesus stopped the funeral procession and, laying his hand on the coffin, said to the dead, "Young man, arise!" And the young man arose, and Jesus delivered him to his mother. That great miracle at Shunem must have been a prophecy of the power of Christ one day to heal all broken hearts and to restore to every mother her lost child.

But what I wish to center upon in this noble narrative about the great woman of Shunem and the child which she got, lost, and got again, is that word which the child's father spoke to the reapers when the child suffered a sunstroke that morning in the fields—"Carry him to his mother."

"Carry him to his mother!" Who is there now, a grown man, who does not have some recollection of being carried to his mother? When you stubbed your toe, when the dog bit you, or you fell out of the haymow, or you had a sunstroke, they carried you to your mother. She knew best how to comfort and soothe and bind up. It was good to be carried to mother. Some speak rather lightly of Mother's Day as just a bath of emotionalism and sentimentalism, as if all mothers were good and godly like this Shunammite mother whose boy fell sick in the harvest fields. It may indeed be sentiment, but it is a mighty wholesome sentiment. It will do everyone good to be carried to his mother.

I. CARRY HIM TO HIS MOTHER WHEN HIS FAITH IN GOD IS HURT

The world makes war on a man's faith, and conspires to steal it away from him. The loss of faith is the most serious of all losses, and the deepest of all hurts. Therefore, when a man's faith is hurt or shaken, carry him to his mother. This Shunammite woman was a woman of great faith before she was a mother. When trouble came she knew where to go. When this child came into the world, miraculously given to her and her husband, he found waiting for him that greatest advantage which can fall to an immortal soul when it comes first into this world —a godly, believing mother.

If a man's faith is shaken, that is the thing to do —carry him to his mother. What is said about a mother's prayer and a mother's Bible is far more than sentiment; it is a deep and powerful reality. One of the greatest and most gifted of the defenders of Christianity was Chateaubriand, the author of the famous book, *The Genius of Christianity*. This tribute of Chateaubriand to Christianity is all the more striking because he himself was a man who lapsed from the Christian faith and afterward returned to it. He had written a book in which he

[180]

had expressed the most skeptical ideas. He had said that reason would not permit him to believe in the immortality of the soul, and that we should have no desire to outlive our ashes. But about that time he received word of the death on May 31, 1798, of his mother. This mother was a woman who had renounced the vanities and shows of his high social position and had devoted herself to religion. In the letter from his sister which informed him of his mother's death, Chateaubriand was reminded of the many tears his beloved mother had shed over his errors, and how she had prayed that his eyes might be opened, and that he would give up his writings against the Christian faith.

This affliction, and the subsequent death of his devout sister also, wrought a complete change in the heart and mind of Chateaubriand. Describing this change, Chateaubriand said in a celebrated phrase, "I wept and I believed." The result of his change of heart was that he now devoted the pen which had written against Christianity, to defend it and to praise it. The result was his superb work *The Genius of Christianity*. What had happened to Chateaubriand? Affliction had carried him to his mother, and to his mother's God. "I wept and I believed."

There was a man who once was assailed by an atheist. He plied him with argument after argument, and many of them apparently unanswerable, as he sought to undermine the foundations of his faith. After a brilliant and effective argument, the atheist exclaimed to the man, "Now what have you left?" He answered, "My mother's life." Yes, that is a great and unanswerable answer! "Carry him to his mother."

II. CARRY A MAN TO HIS MOTHER IN THE HOUR OF TEMPTATION

In the hour of temptation there is no stronger barrier between a man and sin than the memory of a godly mother or father. A great preacher and evangelist of a decade or two ago related how one night he was going out with evil companions to a place of disrepute. It would have been his first departure from the path of innocence; but on the way he had a sudden vision of his father's face—the godly father who had put his arm around him and said, "My boy, it would kill me if you went wrong." The recollection of his father saved him from his temptation, and from scarring his soul with a scar which time could never erase.

Every man and woman knows that this is not sentiment, but real and beautiful and profound truth— the saving influence of the memory of a godly father or mother. Harriet Beecher Stowe, writing of

[182]

the mother of the Beechers—that extraordinary family—said:

I think it will be the testimony of all her sons that her image stood between them and the temptations of youth, as a sacred shield, and that the hope of meeting her in heaven has sometimes been the last strand which did not part during the hours of temptation, and that the remembrance of her holy life and death was a solemn witness to the truth of religion, which repelled every assault of skepticism and drew back the soul from ever wandering to the faith which she lived and died.

The great actor Edwin Forrest, when asked how he had come unscathed through the temptations of the theater, said: "True, I have had temptations; nor have I always resisted them on the instant. The moment, however, when I was on the point of becoming the inebriate, or the gambler, and disgracing my profession, the words of my mother came up angel-like and checked me in my career."

Yes, in the time of temptation, carry a man to his mother. "Three times," wrote a man to me, "the memory of my mother has kept me from crime."

III. WHEN A MAN HAS BEEN HURT BY SIN, CARRY HIM TO HIS MOTHER

When a man has wandered from God and virtue, then carry him to his mother. Lay his scarred and stained soul in her arms, for she will never despair of him. She will have faith in his spiritual recovery; as the Shunammite woman did in the physical recovery of that sick child, now dead, whom she laid on Elisha's bed.

Sometimes about the only place we can carry a sin-stained soul is to his mother. Others may scorn him or refuse him or abandon him; but not his mother. The warden of one of our great penitentiaries says that the mother is the one who holds on to a prisoner to the last. First his friends fall away; then his brothers and sisters; then his children, if he has any; and then the wife, if the prisoner is a man, or the husband, if the prisoner is a woman. All of them fall away and cease to write letters and cease to visit. But the mother holds on to the last. In that respect she illustrates the infinite patience and mercy of God. Carry the sinning man to his mother. The very thought of her righteous life, or her unfailing prayers, may bring him back to God. It may bring him back to God, if it is the influence of a living mother; and still more—mysteriously and beautifully so—if the mother's influence is an influence which shines like a star from the other world. "Carry him to his mother."

This is a word not only to sons and daughters, but also to mothers—the mothers of today, and the young women who are to be mothers tomorrow. Are you living so that when your child comes he will find a woman of faith waiting for him? And mothers of today, are you living so that when your son is losing his faith, or is tempted to sin, or has fallen into sin, the recollection of you and your character, and your faith, will strengthen him and deliver him and save him? Are you the sort of mother of whom they can say, "Carry him to his mother"?

And this is a word, too, for all sons and daughters, both young and old. God's Holy Spirit is speaking to you. Do you remember what the greatest of all mothers said of the greatest of all sons—"Whatsoever he saith unto you, do it"? That is the word that we speak and repeat now. It is the word that your godly mother would say unto you. "Whatsoever *He* saith unto you"—that is, the Lord Jesus Christ—"Whatsoever *He* saith unto you, do it." "Carry him to his mother."

If God has been speaking to any son or daughter through these words, then do what he says.

> O Mother, when I think of thee,
> 'Tis but a step to Calvary;
> Thy gentle hand upon my brow
> Is leading me to Jesus now.

XII

THE WOMAN WHO TOUCHED HIM

"And Jesus said, Who touched me?"
LUKE 8:45

IN THE GOSPELS WE HAVE THE RECORD OF SIX PER-
sons whom Jesus touched, and who were healed by
that touch of divine power and compassion. But here
we have it the other way. Here is one who touched
Jesus and was healed.

Like the play within the play in Hamlet, what we
have here is a miracle within a miracle. You might
call it a wayside miracle—just an episode in the rais-
ing from death of the daughter of the ruler of the
synagogue at Capernaum. And yet the more one
contemplates this episode, the more wonderful and
beautiful it seems, until one almost loses sight of
that other, and greater, miracle. Jairus, a ruler of
the synagogue, had gone to Jesus to ask him to heal
his little daughter, who was "at the point of death."
Since the scribes and Pharisees and the rulers of the
synagogue were, as a class, hostile to Jesus, it must
have taken considerable courage and humility for this
prominent citizen of Capernaum to go to Jesus and

ask him to heal his daughter. But he loved this child, who was an only child; not an only son this time, as so often in the Bible stories, but an only daughter. He had called in the most reputable and famous physicians; but none of them could do anything for his little daughter, and it was plain that she was going to die unless a miracle took place. So he put aside his pride and went to Jesus. Falling at his feet—which shows how greatly distressed he was—he besought Jesus to come to his house and save the life of his little girl. "Come," he said, "and lay thy hand upon her, and she shall live."

This was an urgent case, and one that required immediate action; so Jesus rose up at once and followed him. When he got word of the sickness of Lazarus, he waited three days before he went to Bethany. But now he rises up immediately to go to the ruler's home. The word quickly spread that Jesus was going to the ruler's house to heal his sick daughter. Some had heard that the daughter was already dead, and they were all excitement to see if Jesus could work so stupendous a miracle as to raise one from the dead. Everywhere people left their houses and shops and joined in the procession that was marching toward the mansion of the chief ruler of the synagogue.

Among those who heard that Jesus was on the way to the house of Jairus was an unfortunate woman. Since Jesus called her "daughter," she must still have been a young woman; but hard labor and sorrow and the drain of her disease had withered the flower of her youth. For twelve years she had suffered from a hemorrhage. This grievous disease not only weakened her body and depressed her spirits, but made her a social outcast. If she was a married woman she was compelled to leave her husband. She could not go up to the Temple and the place of sacrifices. If she touched any object or any person, that object and that person were defiled. If any other person touched her, that person was thereby made unclean.

Such was the sad and terrible plight of this unfortunate woman. She had gone to one physician after another, who took her money but could effect no cure. Mark says that she "had spent all that she had, and was nothing bettered, but rather grew worse." Twelve years had passed. Think of all the things you have done, the places you have gone, the sights you have seen, and the joys you have had in twelve years! But the only experience of this poor woman was to see her strength and health wasting away and her fortune completely consumed in vain efforts to be healed.

But this day she was on the street there in the midst of the crowd at Capernaum, for she had heard that Jesus was on his way to heal the daughter of

Jairus. There you can see her, crouching against the wall, trying to make herself as inconspicuous as possible, lest someone should recognize her and order her away. She had heard things concerning Jesus. We have to hear things about Christ before we can go to him and be healed. That was what Paul meant when in that great passage he said, "Whosoever shall call upon the name of the Lord shall be saved. How then shall they call on him in whom they have not believed? and how shall they believe in him of whom they have not heard? and how shall they hear without a preacher?"

The preachers in this case had been the neighbors and friends this woman had heard speak about Jesus. Through them she had heard that he had raised up Peter's mother-in-law, that he had healed a nobleman's son, and the slave of the Roman centurion; and now she heard that he was on his way to raise up the daughter of Jairus. Now a flicker of hope lights up her soul. If you and I had been there, and had seen her crouching against the wall with downcast countenance, we might have seen in her face and in her eyes at least a faint reflection of that hope and that light. And there she stands, waiting, waiting, and hoping that he might pass that way. How many there are like this woman—just waiting, just hoping. Move carefully, speak gently, act kindly; for someone there where you are passing is just waiting and hoping.

But now she hears the stir of the multitude and the trampling of many feet; the boys, as usual, running ahead of the crowd, and crying shrilly one to another. Presently she sees Jesus approaching. He is walking beside Jairus, who is arrayed in his rich robes of the ruler, and other elders of the synagogue and prominent people are about him. The crowd presses close behind, and on either side, and walks in front of Jesus. He and the ruler are walking rapidly, for time is valuable because the little girl is at the point of death.

Now watch this woman against the wall, as she lifts her head and looks eagerly in the direction of Jesus. She is talking to herself, and this is what she is saying: "If I do but touch his garment, I shall be made whole. And yet, do I dare to try it? How can I get through this great crowd, when I am so weak and frail, and hardly able to stand? If the rulers see me, will they let me approach him? After all, I am only an outcast; but so were the lepers; they were unclean too, and yet I hear that he healed them. He is on his way, also, to the house of a rich man. Perhaps he will not care to heal a poor woman like me, for I have spent all I had on the physicians, and have nothing with which to pay him. And yet I have heard that he takes pity on the poor."

Thus alternate waves of hope and despair rolled over the soul of this woman. But Jesus was passing, passing, passing! Soon he would be gone, and her chance would be gone too. Summoning up her courage, she resolves to try to touch him. She steps out into the crowd on the street and works her way through the throng, fearful every moment lest someone will rebuke her and send her back. But at length she gets close behind Jesus. Every loyal Jew wore four tassels on his garment, bound in blue. These hung from the four corners of the robe—one at each side, one in front, and one behind. This was the hem of the garment. Now the woman puts out her hand quickly and touches that tassel which hangs down behind. Instantly, the feeling of weakness and sickness to which she has awakened every day for the last twelve years leaves her, and in its place comes the delightful, indescribable surge of health. She knows immediately that she has been healed.

When Christ healed the woman, she knew it. When great changes come over your body, you know it. And when great changes come over the heart and the soul, you will know it.

With a great joy in her heart the woman hastily turns away to lose herself in the crowd, and is on her way back to the wall again when the crowd around her suddenly stands still, and she with them, for Jesus has stopped. She trembles in her heart as she hears Jesus ask that question, as he looks about him over the crowd, "Who touched me?" "Will he find out," she thinks to herself, "that I touched him? will he think that my touch has made him unclean, and will he punish me because of that?" Then, in a moment, she feels a degree of relief as she hears the people around Jesus say, "Lord, none of us touched thee," and then Peter's loud ringing voice, saying, "Master, the multitude throng thee and press thee, and sayest thou, Who touched me?" But Jesus answers, "No; that is not it. I was not thinking of the press of the multitude. It was a different kind of touch. Someone hath touched me. Who touched me?"

All the time you can imagine the distress of Jairus; you can see the look of anxiety on his face, as he thinks of that little daughter at the point of death. Perhaps he said to Jesus, "Master, why do you stand here arguing about some invisible person who touched you, when my little daughter is at the point of death? Oh, Master, come quickly with me, else my daughter die!" But wait, anxious Jairus, wait! What Christ does here for this woman will give thee faith in his power to heal, to raise from the dead, when presently that terrible word comes to thee that thy daughter is dead and thy neighbors say to thee, "Trouble the Master no more."

The poor woman, certain that she cannot be hid and

that Jesus will know who touched him, and that she will be exposed, comes trembling and falls down before him, and tells him why she has touched him and how she has been healed. After she has told the story of her sickness and her faith and her healing touch, Jesus says to her, "Daughter." She is the only woman, as far as we know, who was thus addressed by Jesus. He calls her "daughter"—the same tender word which the rich ruler, Jairus, used when he asked Jesus to come and heal his little daughter. It was a word of encouragement and of affection. "Daughter, be of good comfort: thy faith hath made thee whole; go in peace." That, you know, was what Jesus said to the unknown woman who washed his feet with her tears and dried them with the hair of her head—"Go in peace." "It was not the hem of my garment that you touched that healed you; but your faith in me hath made you whole. Go in peace."

CHRIST AND THE INDIVIDUAL

This beautiful story shows, first of all, the interest that Jesus took in the individual. His public ministry was brief, and great was the work that he had to do and the truths he had to declare; yet he always had time for the individual, for the one who was in need, and for the one who sought after him. He saw Zacchaeus the publican there in the top of the sycamore tree, outside the gate at Jericho, and told him to come down. Although so many other voices were calling and shouting that day by the gate at Jericho, he heard the cry of the blind beggar, Bartimaeus, "Have mercy on me," and stopped and called him to him and opened his eyes. Yes, Christ was always on the lookout for the individual. At the very last, when he hung on the cross, he stopped dying for mankind long enough to talk with a thief and take him to heaven with him. You may feel that no one is interested in you, that no man careth for your soul; but you are mistaken. There is One who cares; there is One who is deeply interested in you, and that is he who died for you on the Cross.

Once more, this miracle shows us how faith heals. Was it superstition—this touching of the hem of his garment? Was her act like that of the people in Jerusalem who laid their sick along the street, so that when Peter passed by at least his shadow might fall over them? Was it like those people at Ephesus who brought to their sick friends handkerchiefs and aprons which Paul had touched with the hope that thus they might be healed? It probably was; and yet in her touch there was faith. She did not try to touch the hem of the garment of Jairus, or any of the rulers or notables who were in that procession that day; but only the hem of the garment of Jesus. Prayer, the Bible, worship, the sacraments of the church—all these are, as it were, the hem of his garment; and if you have faith, if you are seeking the Christ who is back of them, your touch on these things will have healing and cleansing power.

Again, this woman, when she had been healed, told the whole story and confessed to the healing power of Jesus; so that not only Christ and Jairus, but all the people heard it. If some touch on the hem of Christ's garment has blessed you and helped you, then tell it; for your telling of it may encourage some other to come from behind in the press of the crowd and touch his garment. I have not the slightest doubt that this woman's story had great influence upon Jairus. Jesus had no sooner finished speaking with the woman than the messengers came from the house of Jairus and said to the ruler, "Thy daughter is dead; trouble not the Master." But Jesus, hearing that, said to Jairus, "Fear not; only believe, and she shall be made whole." I am sure that it was easier for Jairus to believe and trust that Jesus could raise his daughter, even from the grave, because of what that woman had told about the healing touch on the hem of Christ's garment.

Who touched me? Many today are thronging the churches. Many today are thronging Christ. But who will touch him with the touch of faith? Yes, I am sure there are those at this very moment who greatly need to touch him. Some one of you has an old sorrow that has been draining your strength—for a month, for a year, for twelve years, perhap longer. In another's heart is some dread or fear that has hung over you like a dark cloud. In some other heart is dislike, or enmity, or hatred, which tears your soul. Someone is beset by an ugly appetite that defiles body and soul. Someone is troubled and haunted by the memory of the transgressions of yesterday. Yes; there are many today who need him, many who need to touch him. I am sure that as we have been considering this woman's story some of you have been saying within yourselves, as she did there against the wall in Capernaum when Jesus was passing by, "If I do but touch his garment, I shall be made whole." And what you say within yourself, to your soul, is true. Christ is still here; the healing of his seamless dress is in our midst.

I sometimes wonder what became of that robe of Jesus, with its four tassels of blue—that one which this woman touched. No doubt it was the very robe over which the Roman soldiers cast lots and threw their dice when Jesus hung dying on the Cross. One of those soldiers threw the lucky number and got the robe of Jesus and carried it off to his home. Perhaps he wore it himself when he was pensioned from the army, or perhaps it was made into garments for his children. What happened to that robe after the Roman soldier won it, no one can tell. Yes; I can tell you now. That same robe is in our midst.

Crowds have thronged him; who will touch him? Who will touch him, now? Would you not like to stretch forth your hand and touch him now? "Jesus of Nazareth passeth by!" That woman heard that cry that day in Capernaum. It was her first and last chance. In a moment he would have passed by and been lost to her—perhaps forever; but while he was passing, and before he had passed, she overcame her doubts and her fears, and stretched forth her hand and touched him, and was made whole. She heard him say, "Daughter, be of good comfort: thy faith hath made thee whole; go in peace." Would you not like to hear him say that to you at this moment? Will you stretch forth your hand now and touch him?

XIII

THE IDEAL WOMAN

"Thou excellest them all."
PROVERBS 31:29

IN THE DAYS WHEN THE CZARS STILL RULED IN
Russia, I once paid a visit to Peterhof, the summer
home of the Czars, and not far from St. Petersburg.
At that time it was a beautiful and attractive country palace, with fountains in the gardens rivaling
those of Versailles. In one of the chambers of the
palace the walls and the ceiling were completely covered with portraits of beautiful women, favorites of
the Czars who lived there. But the Bible is the greatest portrait gallery in the world. The famous galleries such as Dresden, the Rycks Museum at Ams-
terdam, the Louvre at Paris, the National Gallery at
London, and Pitti Gallery at Florence cannot com-
pare for a moment with the gallery of Old Testament
and New Testament paintings; and very notable is
the Bible's gallery of female portraits.

In this series of sermons we have taken our journey through the Biblical gallery of women, where
we have looked on the faces of Ruth, Esther, Rahab,

Martha, Mary, Delilah, Abigail, Rebekah, Rachel, and others whose names are unknown. What a great thing it would be if we could have a composite portrait which would unite the fascination of Delilah, the decision of Ruth, the beauty of Rachel, the ambition of Rebekah, the faith of Rahab, the eloquence of Abigail, the efficiency of Martha, and the pious meditation of Mary. Fortunately, we have the Ideal Woman painted for us in the last chapter of the Book of Proverbs. Here we have the words that King Lemuel learned from his mother, warning him against strong drink and the wrong kind of women. But the book comes to a close with a hymn in praise of Ideal Womanhood. We cannot be sure, but perhaps King Lemuel was describing his own mother. Many a man would think of his own mother as he reads this immortal passage. I knew of a minister who used to tell me how his father would sometimes read this chapter at family worship, then close the Bible before kneeling in prayer and, looking around the family circle, say, "Boys, there's your mother."

This king wanted to know where he could find a virtuous woman. Now he has found her, and here is her description and portrait.

I. HER INDUSTRY

"She looketh well to the ways of her household,

and eateth not the bread of idleness." The bread of idleness, upon which so many women feed, is the source of much weakness and evil in their life. One has defined a popular perversion of Christianity as "imagination working on idleness." But here is a woman whose candle goeth not out by night. That burning candle is a symbol of the sacrificial life of a good woman.

> I love to think her like a blessed candle
> Burning through life's long night;
> Greatly useful, simple, gentle, tender,
> Always giving light.

In George Eliot's *Clerical Sketches* there is a fine description of the faithful wife of the rector, Amos Barton, lighting her candle at early morning and attacking the heap of stockings at her side.

Mrs. Barton carried up-stairs the remainder of her heap of stockings, and laid them on a table close to her bedside, where also she placed a warm shawl, removing her candle, before she put it out, to a tin socket fixed at the head of her bed. Her body was very weary, but her heart was not heavy, in spite of Mr. Woods the butcher, and the transitory nature of shoe-leather; for her heart so overflowed with love, she felt sure she was near a fountain of love that would care for husband and babes better than she could foresee; so she was soon asleep. But about half-past five in the morning, if there were any angels watching round her bed—and angels might be glad of such an office—they saw Mrs. Barton rise up quietly, careful not to disturb the slumbering Amos, who was snoring the snore of the just, light her candle, prop herself upright with the pillows, throw the warm shawl round her shoulders, and renew her attack on the heap of undarned stockings.

"She riseth while it is yet night." How many sons and daughters will remember that—how their mother rose before it was day and had their breakfast ready for them as they started out on the battle of a new day. Many years ago I paid a visit in Edinburgh to Alison Cunningham, the faithful nurse of Robert Louis Stevenson—the one to whom he owed such a debt of gratitude for having led him safely through his early years of sickness, and who impressed upon his mind great moral and spiritual truths. It was to her that he dedicated his volume *A Child's Garden of Verses* in these lines:

> For the long nights you lay awake
> And watched for my unworthy sake:
> For your most comfortable hand
> That led me through the uneven land:
> For all the story-books you read:
> For all the pains you comforted:
> For all you pitied, all you bore,
> In sad and happy days of yore:—
>
> .   .   .   .
>
> From the sick child, now well and old,
> Take, nurse, the little book you hold!

And grant it, Heaven, that all who read
May find as dear a nurse at need,
And every child who lists my rhyme,
In the bright, fireside, nursery clime,
May hear it in as kind a voice
As made my childish days rejoice!

II. HER LOYALTY

The Ideal Woman is loyal to her husband and to her children. "The heart of her husband doth safely trust in her. . . . . She will do him good and not evil all the days of her life." Her husband is "known in the gates." She faithfully forwards him in all things good, in contrast with other women and wives, who frequently are a hindrance to the success and advancement of their husbands. Some of the noblest chapters in human relationships are those which relate to fidelity of wives to distinguished husbands. On the grave of Jane Welsh in Haddington Churchyard, Thomas Carlyle, who suffered remorse because he felt that he had not been always mindful of the treasure he had in that wife, put these words:

For forty years she was the true and loving helpmate of her husband, and by act and word unweariedly forwarded him as none else could in all of worthy that he did or attempted. She died at London, 21st April 1866, suddenly snatched from him, and the light of his life as if gone out.

"She will do him good all the days of her life." Not just a romantic flash at the beginning of their relationship; but, clear down to the very end, a love that never tires.

And that same Stevenson wrote of his wife:

> Trusty, dusky, vivid, true,
> With eyes of gold and bramble-dew,
>   Steel-true and blade-straight,
> The great artificer
> Made my mate.

What can surpass the loyalty of a good wife or mother? The author of that terrifying book *Out of the Night*, amid all his wanderings and transgressions, cherished the memory of his godly mother. He tells us how his mother sold the family silver and bought for him sea boots, blankets, oilskins, and gave him a small Bible as he was about to go to sea. When they parted at Hamburg he saw her last at the train window, "shabby, frail, sad, and invincibly loyal."

III. HER CHARITY

"She stretcheth out her hand to the poor; yea, she reacheth forth her hands to the needy." Sometimes women are sacrificial and self-denying at home with their families, but outside of the home are hard and unfeeling. But this woman stretched forth her hands to the poor and the needy. She was like that

Dorcas of whom we read in the Book of Acts, and whom Peter raised from the dead. "This woman was full of good works and almsdeeds which she did." When Peter came to her home at Joppa, he found all the widows mourning over her, and they showed him the coats and garments which Dorcas made "while she was with them." Yes, the tears of the poor are the best epitaph of the dead.

One of the clearest memories that I have of Christmas at home is the recollection of how our mother sent me and my brother across the river one Christmas morning to a humble home in a poor settlement, where we left a basket of supplies for the family. I think I learned that morning the truth of the beautiful saying of our Lord, which was saved and recovered for us by Paul in his farewell address at Miletus to the elders of the church of Ephesus— how it is "more blessed to give than to receive."

IV. THE BEAUTY OF HER SPEECH

"The law of kindness is on her tongue." On an old tombstone in Egypt was found this epitaph: "Peace was in the words which came from his mouth, and the book of the wise was on his tongue." In his account of the women of Laputa, how they raised an insurrection when it was proposed that henceforth speech be abandoned and that all communication be with signs, Dean Swift takes a jibe at woman's fondness for speech. He might have said the same thing about men. Yet, where the tongue is wrongly used, woman probably has the pre-eminence over man. In his famous description of the tongue, James calls it "a world of iniquity," which "setteth on fire the course of nature; and it is set on fire of hell." But here is a woman with the law of kindness on her tongue. No ill report gains an inch of territory through her passing it on to another. She does not impute wrong motives to others. She thinketh no evil and rejoiceth not in iniquity, but rejoiceth in the truth. Where praise is possible, she praises; and where it is not possible, she keeps silence. Well do I remember my mother's comment on an unworthy person who was being discussed: "Yes, but one of those souls for whom Christ died."

V. HER GODLY CHARACTER

"A woman that feareth the Lord, she shall be praised." Was she a beautiful woman? Nothing is said about that; but all the better if these lovely traits were framed in a beautiful body, for the charm of womanly beauty will last as long as the charm of a beautiful sunrise or the morning glory of roses in June. What is emphasized here is another kind of beauty—the beauty of soul. Strength and honor are this woman's clothing. Bodily beauty is vain and deceitful. It may become the ally and agent of evil and temptation; and even where it is united with a beautiful soul it is bound to fade and vanish despite all the artifices of the beauty parlor. But the beauty of the soul never fades, and never leads astray or deceives.

Before we bid farewell to this Ideal Woman, we might attempt a brief paraphrase of this hymn in her praise in the Book of Proverbs. "A virtuous woman, who can find? But the worldly woman you can find anywhere today. Her name is legion. The virtuous woman riseth while it is night to engage in her labors for the family, but the worldly woman riseth sometime before noon. The candle of the virtuous woman goeth not out by night, but the cigaret of the worldly woman goeth not out by day or night. She layeth her hand to the cards, and her hand holdeth the cocktail. Her husband searcheth for her at the picture shows. She openeth her mouth with folly, and on her tongue is the law of gossip."

But here is another kind of woman. "Thou excellest them all." Her influence abides from generation to generation, and her children rise up and call her blessed. The uplifting, preserving, warning, sanctifying, purifying, and comforting influence of a godly mother is one of the most powerful forces that work upon the soul of man. Well could Paul appeal to Timothy by the faith and love of his mother Eunice and his grandmother Lois. A great preacher of a bygone generation, T. DeWitt Talmadge, used to tell how when his father was absent from the New Jersey farm home, his mother would take his father's place at the family altar, and would always pray that all her children might be the "subjects of converting grace." Name, if you can, a higher, stronger, more uplifting, and more abiding influence than that of a good mother!

This ancient sketch of the Ideal Woman was written before Christ came. Now the Christian artist can add a few strokes of his own with the New Testament brush; and there you have the complete masterpiece. Make her a woman who has bowed at the Cross; make her a woman who loves the church which Christ loved and for which he shed his precious blood; make her a woman whose Eternal Lover is the Lord Jesus Christ, and there you have the Ideal Christian Woman.

Would you women of today know the highest joy in life? Would you repeat and renew yourself, and have yourself go on from generation to generation? Then join the company of those women who followed Christ when he was on earth and ministered unto him, and who, when he was dead, brought their myrrh and spices to anoint his body.

GREAT WOMEN OF THE BIBLE

CLARENCE E. MACARTNEY

In other volumes Dr. Macartney has proved his biographical power by preaching on great men of the Bible, but only recently did he yield to popular request for sermons on the great women of that Book which he knows so well. To prepare, he gave his congregation the opportunity of voting on the greatest women of the Bible, just as they had voted on the greatest men. Ruth stood first; Eve came last. Most of the women in this volume were near the top of the list, though Dr. Macartney himself has added several who did not win places among the first ten "elected." One of those added is not a good but a bad woman, because, says Dr. Macartney, "no series on women of the Bible would be complete without a sermon on such a person as Delilah, the temptress of Samson."

These sermonic biographies—or biographic sermons—are full of ideas, of pen pictures, of applications to life. Each is an unforgettable portrait, written with a profound understanding of the human spirit and of its life-problems. Here are history-conscious sermons, practical illustrations of abstract principles, shrewd analyses, appreciative tributes, inspiring meditations drawn from life. The reader may learn much from these studies, for they contain a truly practical spiritual wisdom. The great women of the Bible have given the preacher what he calls "an unsurpassed opportunity to press home upon the people the claims of Christ as Friend and Redeemer."

"What a great thing," says the author, "it would be if we could have a composite portrait which would unite the fascination of Delilah, the decision of Ruth, the beauty of Rachel, the ambition of Rebekah, the faith of Rahab, the eloquence of Abigail, the efficiency of Martha, and the pious meditation of Mary." The "Ideal Woman" he finds painted for us in the last chapter of Proverbs. But his own book is "a composite portrait," done in careful and sympathetic detail. Here is the womanhood of the Bible, vitally, practically, charmingly presented.

ABINGDON PRESS